Praise for *Solving Disproportionality and Achieving Equity* by Edward Fergus

Throughout the country, a growing number of educators have come to the realization that disproportionality in the placement of children of color in special education, and in school discipline practices, is a vital equity issue that must be confronted. In this important new book, Dr. Edward Fergus explains why this issue is so important, and he shows what educators can do to solve the problem. Through careful analysis of data obtained from real cases, he shows how the problem is manifest and how it can be thoughtfully addressed. For educators and policy makers seeking solutions to these complex issues, this book will be an invaluable resource.

—**Pedro Noguera, Distinguished Professor of Education**
UCLA, Graduate School of Education and Information Studies
Los Angeles, CA

Solving Disproportionality and Achieving Equity addresses burning and significant needs and issues in the field, including areas in which districts are facing legal requirements for action. The synthesis of research, theory, and application, with an acknowledgment of the interpersonal and emotional dimensions of this work, all contribute to its value.

—**Gary Bloom, Senior Program Consultant**
New Teacher Center
San Francisco Bay Area, CA

I believe that this text has the potential to become a bible for every school leader who truly wants to examine the inequities in schools and then move forward with a comprehensive plan applying a sound analysis of the data.

—**William A. Howe, Educator**
Connecticut State Department of Education
Hartford, CT

D1073620

Solving
Disproportionality
and Achieving Equity

I dedicate this book to all the adults who are unapologetic about championing the need for humanity in how we create protective environments for our kids, particularly kids who experience vulnerable conditions!

Solving Disproportionality and Achieving Equity

A Leader's Guide to Using Data to Change Hearts and Minds

Edward Fergus

CORWIN
A SAGE Publishing Company

FOR INFORMATION:

Corwin

A SAGE Company

2455 Teller Road

Thousand Oaks, California 91320

(800) 233-9936

www.corwin.com

SAGE Publications Ltd.

1 Oliver's Yard

55 City Road

London EC1Y 1SP

United Kingdom

SAGE Publications India Pvt. Ltd.

B 1/I 1 Mohan Cooperative Industrial Area

Mathura Road, New Delhi 110 044

India

SAGE Publications Asia-Pacific Pte. Ltd.

3 Church Street

#10-04 Samsung Hub

Singapore 049483

Program Director: Dan Alpert

Senior Associate Editor: Kimberly Greenberg

Editorial Assistant: Katie Crilley

Production Editor: Melanie Birdsall

Copy Editor: Lana Todorovic-Arndt

Typesetter: C&M Digitals (P) Ltd.

Proofreader: Sally Jaskold

Indexer: Karen Wiley

Cover Designer: Anupama Krishnan

Marketing Manager: Charline Maher

Copyright © 2017 by Corwin

All rights reserved. When forms and sample documents are included, their use is authorized only by educators, local school sites, and/or noncommercial or nonprofit entities that have purchased the book. Except for that usage, no part of this book may be reproduced or utilized in any form or by any means, electronic or mechanical, including photocopying, recording, or by any information storage and retrieval system, without permission in writing from the publisher.

All trademarks depicted within this book, including trademarks appearing as part of a screenshot, figure, or other image, are included solely for the purpose of illustration and are the property of their respective holders. The use of the trademarks in no way indicates any relationship with, or endorsement by, the holders of said trademarks.

Printed in the United States of America

Library of Congress Cataloging-in-Publication Data

Names: Fergus, Edward, author.

Title: Solving disproportionality and achieving equity : a leader's guide to using data to change hearts and minds / Edward Fergus.

Description: Thousand Oaks, California : Corwin, 2017. | Includes bibliographical references and index.

Identifiers: LCCN 2016028956 | ISBN 9781506311258 (pbk. : alk. paper)

Subjects: LCSH: Educational equalization—United States. | Discrimination in education—United States.

Classification: LCC LC213.2 .F45 2017 | DDC 379.2/6—dc23 LC record available at https://lccn.loc.gov/2016028956

This book is printed on acid-free paper.

20 21 22 23 11 10 9

DISCLAIMER: This book may direct you to access third-party content via Web links, QR codes, or other scannable technologies, which are provided for your reference by the author(s). Corwin makes no guarantee that such third-party content will be available for your use and encourages you to review the terms and conditions of such third-party content. Corwin takes no responsibility and assumes no liability for your use of any third-party content, nor does Corwin approve, sponsor, endorse, verify, or certify such third-party content.

Contents

Acknowledgments   xiii

About the Author   xv

Introduction   1

    Changing Landscape of Teaching Force and
       Its Effect on Disproportionality   2
       Special Education Classification   2
       Gifted/AP/Honors Enrollment   3
       Suspensions and Behavioral Referrals   3
    The Backdrop of the Integration Project Framework   6
    Organization of the Book   7

Sample Road Map for Creating an Equity-Driven School   9

Chapter 1. Social Integration and Intensified
    Segregation Leading to Disproportionality   15

    Post–*Brown v. Topeka Board of Education*
       Integration Patterns   16
    Integration Project: Patterns of Student
       Enrollment Demographics   17
    Integration Project: Patterns of Teacher
       and Principal Demographics   20

Chapter 2. Knowing the Bias-Based Beliefs in Disproportionality   29

    Bias-Based Beliefs in Pedagogy and School Practice:
       How Does It Show Up in Schools?   31
    Colorblindness Belief   31
       Vignette 1a: "I'm a good White person."   34
       Vignette 2a: "I want answers in English only."   35
       Vignette 3a: "I don't see anything wrong with the Black
          students playing the role of slaves."   35
       Vignette 4a: "I didn't mean anything by it . . .
          why didn't she say anything to me?"   35
       Vignette 5a: "But our school rules state that they
          have to say Mr. or Ms. when addressing
          a teacher. What's wrong with that?"   36
       Colorblindness Reflection Activity   37

Deficit-Thinking Belief   38
    Vignette 1b: "Teachers need to see
      low-income communities."   39
    Vignette 2b: "Our kids' parents don't believe
      in education, especially college education."   39
    Vignette 3b: "Immigrants don't belong
      in our community."   40
    Deficit-Thinking Reflection Activity   41
Poverty-Disciplining Belief   42
    Vignette 1c: "They need to pull up their
      pants . . . they just aren't serious about
      school and they won't get jobs like that."   43
    Vignette 2c: "We overly discipline our students
      because they are coming from poor conditions."   44
    Vignette 3c: "Isn't the problem of disproportionality
      in special education because they are poor?"   44
    Poverty-Disciplining Reflection Activity   45

**Chapter 3. Leadership Inquiry Skills for
Building Equity Focus**   **47**

Section 1: Understanding Your Data and
  Data System Capacity   47
    Data and Research Analysis Capacity:
      Measuring Your Readiness to Use Data   48
      Activity 1: Software Competency   49
      Activity 2: Assessment Competency   50
      Activity 3: Data Analysis Competency   51
      Activity 4: Infrastructure Competency   53
    Critical Reflection   54
    Closing Reflection   55
Section 2: Practicing Analysis and Interpretation
  of Data: Case Studies   55
    Case Study 1: Recognizing Discipline Patterns   55
    Case Study 2: Suspensions Live in Referrals   56
    Case Study 3: Not as Equally Gifted   59
    Case Study 4: Fixing Academic Referrals Leading
      to Special Education Classification   62
    Case Study 5: High Special Education Classification
      Doesn't Happen Overnight   63
    Case Study 6: Reading About Your Identity
      During Adolescence   65

**Chapter 4. A Process for Identifying Disproportionality
and Building an Equity Plan**   **69**

Step 1: Identifying Your Starting Place   70
Step 2: Root Cause Process for Understanding
  Disproportionality Problems   72

Common Root Causes: Findings From a 10-Year
   Data-Driven RCA Process   74
      Cause 1: Gaps in Curriculum
         and Instructional Implementation
            Disproportionately Affect Struggling Learners   75
      Cause 2: Inconsistent Prereferral Process   77
      Cause 3: Limited Beliefs of Ability   78
Starting the RCA Process: Forming a
   Disproportionality Leadership Team   80
Overview of Disproportionality Data Tools   80
Data Needs for Root Cause Analysis   81
      Exercise 1: Data Inventory for Inquiry   82
      Exercise 2: Sample Data Inventory   83
Root Cause Analysis 1: Disproportionality in
   Special Education Classification   86
Root Cause Analysis 2: Disproportionality in
   Gifted, AP, Honors, and/or Accelerated Programs   100
Root Cause Analysis 3: Disproportionality in
   Discipline and Behavioral Supports   115
Summary of Common Root Causes   133
Step 3: Monitoring Equity Work: 3- to 5-Year
   Span of Work   134
      Part 1: Identify SMART Goal(s) and Indicators   135
      Part 2: Create a Task List   138
      Part 3: Create a Timeline   139
Step 4: Progress-Monitoring Tools: Monthly Data Calendar   142
      Important Considerations   142
      Infrastructure and Process   142
Additional Equity Examinations   154
   Course Grade Worksheets   154
   Reflection   158
   Gradebook Audit   159
   Infrastructure and Process   159

Chapter 5. Building an Equity Belief School Climate   167

Leading Equity Competency 1: Know How to
   Manage Race Dialogues   168
Leading Equity Competency 2: Know How to Manage
   the Comfortable and Uncomfortable Tensions of
   Learning and Practice   169
Stage 1 Activities: Building Universal Equity Principles   170
      Activity 1.1: Building Common Definitions
         of Educational Equity   171
      Activity 1.2: Practicing Applying Definitions
         of Educational Equity   172
      Activity 1.3: Creating Schoolwide Equity Principles   173

Stage 2 Activities: Monthly or Quarterly Sessions
    on Bias-Based Beliefs   176
        Deficit Thinking   176
            Activity 2.1a: Unpacking the Deficit-Thinking Elephant   176
            Activity 2.1b: Unpacking the Deficit-Thinking
                Elephant—Survey Activity   177
            Activity 2.2: Replacing the Deficit-Thinking Elephant   178
        Poverty Disciplining   179
            Activity 2.3a Unpacking the Poverty-Disciplining
                Elephant   179
            Activity 2.3b: Unpacking the Poverty-Disciplining
                Elephant—Survey Activity   180
            Activity 2.4: Meritocracy Line   182
            Activity 2.5: Schools Are Protective,
                Not Risk Environments   182
        Colorblindness   184
            Activity 2.6: My First Racial Memory   184
            Activity 2.7: Seeing Your Race-Life Journey   184
            Activity 2.8: Diversity Tables   185
            Activity 2.9a: Replacing Colorblindness Statements   186
            Activity 2.9b: Unpacking the Colorblindness
                Elephant—Survey Activity   187
            Activity 2.10: Promoting Cultural Responsibility Beliefs   188
    Other Ongoing Activities for Replacing Biased Beliefs   189
        Option 1: Video Clip: *Teacher Uses N-Word*   189
        Option 2: Implicit Association Test   189
        Option 3: TED Talks   189
        Option 4: PBS Activities on Race   189
        Option 5: Name Game   190
        Option 6: Understanding Belief Impact on Behavior   190
    Application Activities   192
        Application Activity 1: Affirming Social Identities
            of Kids—Books   192
        Application Activity 2: Affirming Social Identities
            of Kids—Classroom Environment   193
        Application Activity 3: Inserting Demographic
            Criteria in Everyday Practices   193
        Application Activity 4: Adding Culture
            Consciousness and Identity Affirmation Belief
            Into Instructional Practice Texts   194

Appendixes   **197**
    1. Data Inventory Worksheet   198
    2. Planning Sheet for Addressing Beliefs and
       Building Equity Principles   199
    3. Exit Ticket   200
    4. Definitions of Educational Equity Worksheet   201

   5. Applying Definitions of Educational Equity   203
   6. Applying Definitions of Educational Equity:
      Homework Worksheet   204
   7. Building Our Universal Equity Principles Worksheet   205
   8. Shifting Deficit-Thinking Worksheet   206
   9. Shifting Deficit-Thinking Survey Worksheet   208
 10. Definition Flashcards   209
 11. Shifting Poverty-Disciplining
      Belief Statements Worksheet   210
 12. Shifting Poverty-Disciplining
      Belief Statements Survey Worksheet   211
 13. Meritocracy Line Exercise   212
 14. Dual-Axis Model of Vulnerability   214
 15. Dual-Axis Model of Vulnerability Application Worksheet   215
 16. Racial Timeline Worksheet   216
 17. Racial and Ethnic Group Worksheet   219
 18. Shifting Common Colorblindness Statements Worksheet   225
 19. Shifting Common Colorblindness Statements Survey
      Worksheet   226
 20. Cultural Responsibility Beliefs Worksheet   227
 21. Looking at Books Worksheet   228
 22. Observing Classroom Environments Worksheet   229
 23. Equity Resources for Curricular, Culture/Climate,
      and Instruction   230

References   235

Index   241

Acknowledgments

The development of this book is due to the support of several entities in my life: family and friends. My family (nuclear, extended, and in-laws) has been an ever-present champion of this work and what I do. Over 10 years of visiting schools, meeting with staff, and collecting data has only been possible with the love and support of my family—Lorelei, Javier, and Sofia. In particular, my Lorelei, who continuously pushed me to go write this book! Thank you! Also, I cannot talk about my partnership with Lorelei without talking about the spirits that have illuminated our lives: Javier and Sofia have brought new meaning and inspiration to my life in ways that I could never put into words. I am also grateful for my parents, brother Manuel (Manny), and my in-laws (especially Nana!) for being such a super supportive and encouraging family. Among my many friends, there are several that truly help to ground me often—Jamal Cooks, Ines Casillas, Sherri-Ann Butterfield, Kihika Storr, and Pearl Leonard-Rock. Each of you has an uncanny and amazing ability to care for others and share your brilliance with others, being unapologetic about your wonderful personalities. Thank you for being such good friends!

This work came to fruition during my time at the Metropolitan Center for Urban Education, and I am grateful for those who followed my vision for this work. I am also thankful for the many school district staff whom I met over these 10 years; thank you for being such an inspiration and showcasing how practitioners take up the mantle of equity!

PUBLISHER'S ACKNOWLEDGMENTS

Corwin gratefully acknowledges the contributions of the following reviewers:

Trudy Arriaga
Superintendent Ventura Unified
Ventura Unified School District
Ventura, CA

Gary Bloom
Senior Program Consultant
New Teacher Center
San Francisco, CA

William A. Howe
Educator
Connecticut State Department of Education
Hartford, CT

Randall Lindsey
Professor
California State University, Los Angeles
Los Angeles, CA

Sherry Markel
Professor
Northern Arizona University, College of Education,
    Department of Teaching and Learning
Flagstaff, AZ

Vicki Nishioka
Senior Research Advisor, Evaluation
Education Northwest
Portland, OR

Renee Peoples
Teaching and Learning Coach
Swain West Elementary
West Bryson, NC

About the Author

 **Edward Fergus** is assistant professor of educational leadership and policy at Steinhardt School of Culture, Education, and Human Development, New York University. Dr. Fergus's current work is on the intersection of educational policy and outcomes, with a specific focus on Black and Latino boys' academic and social engagement outcomes, disproportionality in special education and suspensions, and school climate conditions. Most recently, he served as deputy director of the Metropolitan Center for Urban Education (2004–2013), a program director at a Children's Aid Society Community School, and later as an education specialist with the Children's Aid Society National Technical Assistance Center (2000–2001 and 2002–2004). He has published numerous articles and is the author of *Skin Color and Identity Formation: Perceptions of Opportunity and Academic Orientation Among Mexican and Puerto Rican Youth* (Routledge Press, 2004), coeditor of *Invisible No More: Disenfranchisement of Latino Men and Boys* (Routledge Press, 2011), and coauthor of *Schooling for Resilience: Improving Trajectory of Black and Latino Boys* (Harvard Education Press, 2014). Dr. Fergus serves on various boards, such as Partnership for Afterschool Education (PASE) and NY State Governor's Juvenile Justice Advisory Group (2010–present), and he was appointed in 2011 to the Yonkers Public Schools Board of Education (2011–2013), and as advisory board member of the Mayor's Leadership Taskforce on Suspension and School Climate (2015–2016), and Young Men's Initiative (2016–present). In addition, Dr. Fergus is an expert consultant for the U.S. Department of Justice Civil Rights Division on Educational Opportunities (2014–present). He also provides consultant support to state education departments on disproportionality state performance plan indicators, specifically development of plans for addressing disproportionality.

Dr. Fergus received a bachelor's degree in political science and education from Beloit College and a doctorate in educational policy and social foundations from the University of Michigan.

Introduction

In 1954, the Supreme Court ruled in *Brown v. Topeka Board of Education* that schools in the United States needed to desegregate and begin integration. The decision was a radical departure from the facilities argument initially presented. More importantly, the *Brown* decision highlighted that the segregation of Black students was having a detrimental effect on their self-concept. Over 60 years later, many scholars argue that integration, as well as the desegregation work, has not been sustained (Ashenfelter et al., 2005; Orfield and Frankenberg, 2014); in fact, a 2014 Civil Rights Project report highlights that Black, Latino, and Native American students are less integrated with White and Asian students today than in 1954 (Orfield & Frankenberg, 2014). For example,

> in a classroom of 30 students, the classmates of the typical White student would include 22 Whites, 2 Blacks, 4 Latinos, 1 Asian and 1 "other" . . . the typical Black or Latino student would have 8 White classmates and at least 20 Black and/or Latino classmates. (p. 12)

Despite this reverse movement in integration, the *Brown v. Topeka Board of Education* decision did set forth another integration project—the integration of White practitioners with Black, Latino, and Native American student populations. Research on the Black teaching force highlights that approximately 38,000 Black teachers were laid off or demoted between 1954 and 1965 (Ethridge, 1979; Holmes, 1990). The implications of this change were twofold: (1) as schools with Black children were viewed as inferior, so were their teachers, which limited the opportunities for them to be hired in White schools, and (2) this change meant Black children and their parents would be entrusting Whites who previously were legally able to live, work, and socialize separately from Blacks. The questions and concerns raised by this historical context include: What are the ways in which this integration affected the educational progress of Black, Latino, and Native American children? How do we equip school leaders with an understanding of the integration project?

This book explores the integration project that has involved social interactions occurring in school environments among racial and ethnic groups with conflicting understandings and experiences of race, ethnicity, gender, and other social identities. Of particular interest is how those understandings and experiences are translated by practitioners into a range of bias-based beliefs premised on these social identities: beliefs such as deficit thinking, colorblindness, and poverty disciplining. And this book is intended to provide for practitioners, specifically leaders, the opportunity to reconstruct the integration project so that it is based on positive understandings of social identities.

CHANGING LANDSCAPE OF TEACHING FORCE AND ITS EFFECT ON DISPROPORTIONALITY

Over the last 60 years, the proportion of White females teaching Black, Latino, and Native American students has increased; the female teacher force grew from 69% in 1986 to 84% in 2011, and from 2004 to 2011, the rate of White teachers has stayed consistent from 83.1% to 81.9%, respectively (National Center on Education Statistics [NCES], 2004, 2011). Additionally, in 2011, among the teaching population, 36% had 10 to 20 years of experience, while 21% had more than 20 years of experience. Among principals in K–12 settings, as recent as 2011–2012, 80% were non-Hispanic White, 10% Black or African American, 7% Hispanic/Latino, and 3% other. In addition, 52% were female and 48% male (Bitterman, Goldring, & Gray, 2013). Meanwhile, the public school enrollment grew decidedly Black and Latino; as of 2011, these two populations comprise 40% of enrollment and are projected to be the majority by 2020 (NCES, 2004, 2011). Furthermore, Black and Latino students specifically are primarily attending schools with only Black and Latino students (NCES, 2004, 2011). These trends demonstrate that White and female teachers are the primary teaching force for Black and Latino children, and a question that needs to be raised is, what are the outcomes of this integration?

The correlated effect of this integration project is noted in research on the achievement and opportunity gap, and disproportionality in special education, gifted/AP/honors programs, and suspension and behavioral referrals. Disproportionality is the over- and underrepresentation of racial/ethnic minority in relation to their overall enrollment (Ahram, Fergus, & Noguera, 2011). Although rates in disproportionality range across the United States, there is a common pattern.

Special Education Classification

In 2011–2012, nationally among the slightly more than 50 million students enrolled in public schools, the racial/ethnic enrollment was the following: White 51.7%, Hispanic 23.7%, Black 15.8%, Asian, 4.7%, and Native American 1.1%. However, the enrollment in special education programs differed greatly from these national patterns. Among the roughly 6 million students with disabilities in 2011–2012, the distribution is distinct across race/ethnicity and gender groups (see Table I.1). Among the students enrolled in special education, 53.1% are White, 21.3% Hispanic/Latino,

19.1% Black, 2.3% Asian, and 1.5% Native American. As expected, a larger percentage of male students are receiving special education services compared to female students, 10.6% and 5.4% respectively. Additionally, Black, White, and Native American males have the largest rates of enrollment in special education services. These patterns highlight a proportional difference between overall enrollment and special education enrollment.

Gifted/AP/Honors Enrollment

Among the roughly 3 million students enrolled in gifted and talented programs in 2011–2012, the distribution is distinct across race/ethnicity and gender groups (see Table I.2). Asian and White males and females maintain the highest proportions enrolled in gifted/talented programs, which means this population has more members enrolled in these programs. Meanwhile, the overall distribution of gifted and talented enrollment is 61% White, 17% Hispanic/Latino, 9.5% Asian, 8.8% Black, and 0.9% Native American.

Suspensions and Behavioral Referrals

Among the 2.8 million students that received at least one in-school suspension, the racial/ethnic disparity is apparent (see Table I.3). Among the population of students receiving in-school suspensions, over 50% are Black and Latino students.

Among the 3 million students receiving one or more out-of-school suspensions in 2011–2012, the pattern also shows Blacks and Latinos comprise more than 50% of the students receiving this consequence (see Table I.4). Of particular interest is the pattern of Black female students nearing 50% of all female students receiving one or more out-of-school suspensions.

Table I.1 Percentage of Students With Disabilities in Public Elementary and Secondary Schools, by Race/Ethnicity and Gender (2011–2012)

	Male	Female	Overall
White	13.3	7.1	53.1
Black	13.5	6.6	19.1
Hispanic/Latino	5.0	2.2	21.3
Asian	2.5	.8	2.3
Native American	9.5	4.6	1.5
English language learner	2.2	0*	9.3
Total	10.6	5.4	

*The numbers are too small and thus are suppressed, and percentage cannot be calculated.

Source: U.S. Department of Education, National Center for Education Statistics, Civil Rights Data Collection (2011–2012)

Table I.2 Percentage of Gifted and Talented Students in Public Elementary and Secondary Schools, by Race/Ethnicity and Gender (2011–2012)

	Male	Female	Overall
White	7.3	7.8	60.8
Black	3.2	4.2	8.8
Hispanic/Latino	4.5	4.8	16.9
Asian	13.0	13.9	9.5
Native American	5.7	6.3	0.9
English language learner	1.9	2.0	2.7
Total	6.2	6.8	

Source: U.S. Department of Education, National Center for Education Statistics, Civil Rights Data Collection (2011–2012)

Table I.3 Percentage of Students Receiving One or More In-School Suspensions in Public Elementary and Secondary Schools, by Race/Ethnicity and Gender (2011–2012)

	Male	Female	Overall
White	41.8	35.2	41.3
Black	29.4	35.8	31.2
Hispanic/Latino	22.9	23.1	22.6
Asian	1.4	1.0	1.0
Native American	1.3	1.5	1.3

Source: U.S. Department of Education, National Center for Education Statistics, Civil Rights Data Collection (2011–2012)

Table I.4 Percentage of Students Receiving One or More Out-of-School Suspensions in Public Elementary and Secondary Schools, by Race/Ethnicity and Gender (2011–2012)

	Male	Female	Overall
White	36.9	29.1	34.5
Black	35.4	44.7	38.2
Hispanic/Latino	22.3	21.2	21.9
Asian	1.2	0.8	1.1
Native American	1.4	1.5	1.4

Source: U.S. Department of Education, National Center for Education Statistics, Civil Rights Data Collection (2011–2012)

Sample Road Map for Creating an Equity-Driven School

		Belief and Awareness Work	Process Change Work	Identifying and Monitoring Equity Work
YEAR 1		**Who:** Entire staff **When:** Monthly staff meetings	**Who:** Intervention or Lead Teacher Teams **When:** Monthly department/grade level/Professional Learning Community meetings	**Who:** Leadership Team **When:** Monthly leadership meetings
	July			Root cause analysis (RCA) sessions
	August	Outline Stage 1 and 2 Activities (ad hoc Equity Team) Share RCA Summary @ School PD	Develop 3- to 5-year Work Plan completion *NOTE:* Two domains of policy/practice root causes may emerge: (1) absent systems/programs (2) misaligned systems/programs Depending on domain, implementation will differ	Develop 3- to 5-year Work Plan (with department heads) RCA Summary
	September	Stage 1, Activity 1.1	Implementation of Work Plan **Domain 1:** Planning and developing of new systems/programs **Domain 2:** Planning and developing of action steps for realignment	Monthly Data Review
	October	Stage 1, Activity 1.2	Implementation of Work Plan **Domain 1:** Planning and developing of new systems/programs **Domain 2:** Planning and developing of action steps for realignment	Monthly Data Review
	November	Stage 1, Activity 1.3	Implementation of Work Plan **Domain 1:** Planning and developing of new systems/programs **Domain 2:** Planning and developing of action steps for realignment	Monthly Data Review and examine fidelity of Work Plan implementation
	December	Stage 2, Activity 2.1a	Implementation of Work Plan **Domain 1:** Planning and developing of new systems/programs **Domain 2:** Planning and developing of action steps for realignment	Monthly Data Review

Chapter 1

Social Integration and Intensified Segregation Leading to Disproportionality

Figure 1.1 Letter to Teacher in Topeka, Kansas

March 13, 1953

Miss Darla Buchanan
623 Western Avenue
Topeka, Kansas

Dear Miss Buchanan:

Due to the present uncertainty about enrollment next year in schools for negro children, it is not possible at this time to offer you employment for next year. If the Supreme Court should rule that segregation in the elementary grades is unconstitutional our Board will proceed on the assumption that the majority of people in Topeka will not want to employ negro teachers next year for White children. It is necessary for me to notify you now that your services will not be needed for next year. This is in compliance with the continuing contract law. If it turns out that segregation is not terminated, there will be nothing to prevent us from negotiating a contract with you at some later date this spring. You will understand that I am sending letters of this kind to only those teachers of negro schools who have been employed during the last year or two. It is presumed that, even though segregation should be declared unconstitutional we would have need for some schools for negro children and we would retain our negro teachers to them. I think I understand that all of you must be under considerable strain, and I sympathize with the uncertainties and inconveniences which you must experience during this period of adjustment. I believe that whatever happens will ultimately turn out to be best for everybody concerned.

Sincerely,

Wendell Godwin, Superintendent of Schools

WG: la

cc: Mr. Whitson Dr. Theilmann Mr. Caldwell

Source: Tillman (2004)

Such letters as in Figure 1.1 represent several dynamics of not only what transpired post–*Brown v. Topeka Board of Education* for Black teachers, but also for White teachers. Practitioners, primarily White teachers, were invited into an integration project involving race, ethnicity, and colorism with limited social experience and interaction with non-White children. This was not the only integration project in the U.S. society. For example, the military integration occurred due to President Truman's Executive Order No. 9981 on July 26, 1948; the order not only declared "that there shall be equality of treatment and opportunity for all persons in the armed services without regard to race, color, religion, or national origin," but also established the President's Committee on Equality of Treatment and Opportunity in the Armed Services. The federal supports for the desegregation of schools took many forms: military presence (e.g., Governor Faubus at Little Rock in 1957; Governor Wallace at University of Alabama in 1963); court mandates of school desegregation in at least 9 out of 17 states with explicit segregation laws; and the Civil Rights Act of 1964 appropriations of technical assistance by Desegregation Assistance Centers for districts to desegregate. Although these various legal actions were a necessary step for removing barriers, they did not contain any provisions for how individuals begin understanding the legacy and effect of racism, nor the capacity to understand future thinking about race, ethnicity, and colorism and their effect. In other words, we have not been able to answer the question bell hooks (1994) asks, "How do you legislate people to get along?" How do we know whether practitioners in general know how to get along with racial/ethnic minority student populations that were previously legally and socially segregated?

POST–*BROWN V. TOPEKA BOARD OF EDUCATION* INTEGRATION PATTERNS

What we know is that historically and currently, all racial and ethnic groups have limited contact with each other. A recent survey report on social networks by Cox et al. (2014) of over 4,000 individuals documents that among White Americans, 91% of their social network are also White, among Black Americans, 83% of their social network are also Black, and among Hispanic Americans, 64% of their social network are also Hispanic. Such information raises concern as to the impact of having limited contact with individuals culturally different than yourself. Having cross-cultural or inter-group experiences, as described by social psychology and anthropology research (Allport, 1954; Cross, 1991; Helms, 1990; Pettigrew, 1979; Pettigrew & Tropp, 2006; Tajfel, 1978), does require intentional personal work; otherwise the absence of this capacity will allow an individual's cultural perspective to dominate interpretation and implementation of school-based practice.

The trend in housing integration is mixed. The U.S. Census Bureau reports (Iceland, Weinberg, & Steinmetz, 2002) demonstrate Black Americans with the highest rates of residential segregation, followed by

Hispanic/Latinos and then Asians during the 1980–2000 period. And more recently, the housing crisis that led to foreclosures between 2005 and 2009 reversed any integration rates; foreclosure rates occurred most acutely among Black, Latino, and racially integrated communities (Hall, Crowder, & Spring, 2015). Additionally the loss of integration was further affected by loss of White population and increases in minority growth.

The absences of integration can also be found in the workplace. Though racial integration has improved compared to the 1960s, there are stark patterns in workforce segregation. Hellerstein and Neumark (2008) in an analysis of employer–employee workforce identified

> extensive segregation by skill in the workplace. . . . For Blacks, the fact that education differences between Blacks and Whites explain virtually none of racial workplace segregation means that further research must be conducted . . . this research necessarily must examine explanations that are not skill based: discrimination, residential segregation, and labor market networks. (p. 476)

Hellerstein and Neumark (2008) cite the segregation between Hispanics and Whites as being partially due to language proficiency; however, a similar examination must occur that considers the other factors named above.

The education research community, meanwhile, systemically developed an evidence pattern in which, as schools become more integrated, bias-based beliefs are ever-present in school environments. Various research studies document the following bias-based belief conditions in schools: race-based ideas of learning and achievement are held by some White teachers toward Black students (Irvine, 1990), and general bias such as deficit thinking, colorblindness, and racial discomfort negatively correlate with a teacher's self-efficacy (Fergus, 2016); the presence of "passive" lowered expectations occurs through interactions such as stereotype threat (Steele & Aronson, 1995) and racial microaggressions (Sue, 2010), and the presence of "active" lowered expectations through school structures such as curriculum (Anyon, 1983) and resource allocation (*Campaign for Fiscal Equity v. New York State*, 2003). Additionally, research documents that the effect of bias can be found in the disproportionate outcomes for Black, Latino, and Native American student populations in achievement, gifted programs, special education, and behavioral referrals and suspensions (e.g., Council of State Governments Justice Center, 2011; Skiba et al., 2011).

INTEGRATION PROJECT: PATTERNS OF STUDENT ENROLLMENT DEMOGRAPHICS

Student enrollment has diversified over the past 25 years. Figure 1.2 demonstrates the percentage of public school enrollment by race/ethnicity between 1988 and 2008. During this 20-year span, the White student

Figure 1.2 Percentage Distribution of Race/Ethnicity Public School Enrollment: 1988–2008

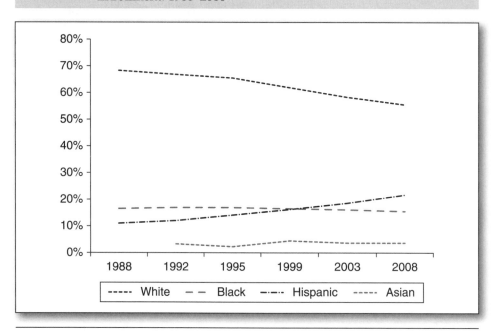

Source: U.S. Department of Commerce, Census Bureau, Current Population Survey (CPS), October Supplement, 1988–2008

enrollment changed from 68.3% to 55.5%. Meanwhile, the Black student enrollment stayed relatively even from 16.5% to 15.5%. However the Hispanic/Latino student enrollment increased dramatically from 11% to 21.7%. This means in most school districts that are experiencing change in enrollment, it is primarily being driven by Hispanic/Latino students.

While the public school enrollment trend is becoming more racially and ethnically diverse, there is a continuing pattern of hypersegregation. Most recently, Orfield and Frankenberg (2014) highlighted several findings: Black and Latino students tend to be in schools with a substantial majority of poor children; Latinos are significantly more segregated than Blacks in suburban schools; and Black and Latino students have low exposure to White students in the largest metropolitan areas and in midsize central cities. Using data from the National Center on Education Statistics, 1995–2006, I demonstrate in various tables the pattern of the hypersegregation. Tables 1.1 through 1.3 provide the percentage of each group's enrollment in public schools with various concentrations of racial/ethnic enrollment minority populations. The overwhelming pattern is that schools are becoming more racially and ethnically segregated for Black, Latino, and Native American populations.

These patterns suggest that Black, Latino, Asian, and Native American students are experiencing higher levels of segregation; in turn, White students are experiencing higher levels of integration compared to all other racial/ethnic groups. The national concern about integration and segregation continuously situates the need to ensure these various populations are

Table 1.1 Percentage of Racial/Ethnic Enrollment Minority Concentration: 1995

	Less than 10% minority	10% to 24% minority	25% to 49% minority	50% to 74% minority	75% to 89% minority	90% or more minority
White	48.5%	23.7%	18.3%	7.3%	1.7%	0.5%
Black	2.6%	8%	21.2%	21.6%	12.5%	34.1%
Hispanic/Latino	2.9%	6.9%	15.5%	21.4%	18.3%	35%
Asian	8.6%	15.7%	22.2%	22.9%	18%	12.7%
Native American	10.6%	19.2%	24.7%	16.4%	7.6%	21.5%

Source: U.S. Department of Education, National Center for Education Statistics, Common Core of Data (CCD), "Public Elementary/Secondary School Universe Survey," 1995–1996, 2000–2001, and 2005–2006

Table 1.2 Percentage of Racial/Ethnic Enrollment Minority Concentration: 2000

	Less than 10% minority	10% to 24% minority	25% to 49% minority	50% to 74% minority	75% to 89% minority	90% or more minority
White	43.4%	25.8%	19.8%	8.2%	2.1%	0.7%
Black	2.3%	7.1%	18.9%	21%	13.3%	37.3%
Hispanic/Latino	2.4%	6.6%	14.7%	20.2%	18.7%	37.5%
Asian	6.9%	15.3%	23%	22%	18.4%	14.5%
Native American	9.2%	18.8%	26.6%	16.8%	8.4%	20.3%

Source: U.S. Department of Education, National Center for Education Statistics, Common Core of Data (CCD), "Public Elementary/Secondary School Universe Survey," 1995–1996, 2000–2001, and 2005–2006

Table 1.3 Percentage of Racial/Ethnic Enrollment Minority Concentration: 2005

	Less than 10% minority	10% to 24% minority	25% to 49% minority	50% to 74% minority	75% to 89% minority	90% or more minority
White	36.8%	27.8%	22.6%	9.4%	2.6%	0.9%
Black	1.9%	6.7%	18.1%	20.9%	14.1%	38.3%
Hispanic/Latino	1.9%	6%	14.4%	19.4%	18.7%	39.5%
Asian	5.1%	14.2%	24.3%	22.1%	18.1%	16.1%
Native American	7.3%	17.0%	27.0%	18.9%	9.3%	20.6%

Source: U.S. Department of Education, National Center for Education Statistics, Common Core of Data (CCD), "Public Elementary/Secondary School Universe Survey," 1995–1996, 2000–2001, and 2005–2006

finding opportunities to be in similar learning environments (Kahlenberg, 2012). Though this should continue to be a necessary policy and practice focus, there should be additional focus on the integration project that continues to grow, as well as the presence of a diversified teaching and principal workforce in front of a diverse student enrollment population, especially Black and Latino student populations.

INTEGRATION PROJECT: PATTERNS OF TEACHER AND PRINCIPAL DEMOGRAPHICS

The conversation on teacher and principal workforce diversity is complex. On one hand, we must consider the historical manner in which racial/ethnic minority populations were placed at various disadvantages to enter this specific workforce. For example, prior to the *Brown v. Board of Education* 1954 decision, upward of 82,000 Black teachers taught approximately two million Black students (Hawkins, 1994); afterward nearly 39,000 Black teachers across 17 states lost their employment between 1954 to 1965 (Cole, 1986; Ethridge, 1979; Holmes, 1990). The loss is tied to schools being required to desegregate, and Black students were primarily moved into predominantly White schools. The explicit discrimination of Blacks continued until the 1964 Civil Rights Act.

A less contemporary reason for the absence of available racial/ethnic minority populations in teaching is the change in opportunities to enter other career fields; in the 1960s, nearly 60% of Black college graduates began careers in teaching within 5 years of graduating (Murnane, Singer, Willett, Kemple, & Olsen, 1991). Additional factors having an effect on the available workforce include the nature of how standardized testing requirements are a main staple of receiving licensure, as well as the nature of content requirements (Madkins, 2011). Though there are a myriad of reasons and labor force changes over the past 30 years, the reduction of racial/ethnic minority teachers fundamentally changed an important school climate dimension, which is the degree to which Black, Latino, and Native American children have teachers familiar with their culture.

The reduction is one component of the integration project concern. The other component involves the nature to which White teachers and principals are themselves prepared to teach and lead a diverse student population that exists within a diverse society. Researcher examination of teacher and principal preparation and related standards establishes a pattern in which attention to diversity, race, culture, and other areas of difference is deafeningly silent. For example, studies of multiculturalism or diversity courses demonstrated positive impact on changing preservice teachers' attitude and belief toward teaching a more diverse learning population (e.g., Lucas & Frazier, 2014; Martin & Dagostino-Kalniz, 2015). Simultaneously, research on principal standards such as Interstate School Leaders Licensure Consortium (ISLLC) and Educational Leadership Program Recognition Standards (ELCC) (Davis, Gooden, & Micheaux,

2015) recently demonstrates a move away from colorblind narrative in the standards used to guide "the traits, functions of work, and responsibilities expected of school and district leaders" (Council of Chief State School Officers, 2008, p. 5). However, though the teacher and principal preparation field has begun to infuse, to a degree, standards on issues of diversity, culture, race, and/or difference in general, the integration project concern is the nature of breadth and depth this work requires given the larger societal apprehension about these issues. Particularly given that teacher preparation usually involves one course on issues of culture and race, our workforce involves individuals with limited contact with individuals culturally and racially different than themselves. So as we consider the demographic trend of teacher and principal populations, we must situate the concern as not solely about the status trend, but also about the nature of how the field considers the training of practitioners needing to include understanding of social integration issues.

In my analysis of teacher and principal racial/ethnic demographic trends, the patterns of integration are clear. The demographics of the teaching and leadership population are different than that of the student population. Figure 1.3 demonstrates the race/ethnicity and gender distribution of full-time teachers between 1987 and 2012. The majority of teachers stayed White and female between 1987 and 2012; over 80% are White, over 70%

Figure 1.3   Percentage of Teachers by Selected Characteristics: 1987–2012

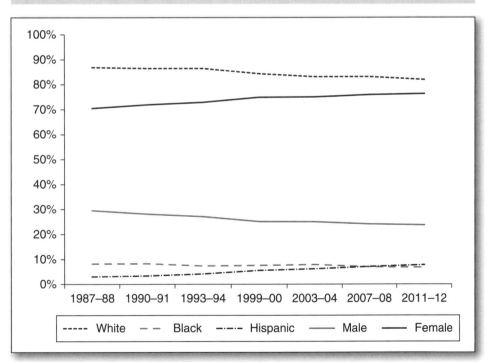

Source: U.S. Department of Education, National Center for Education Statistics, Teacher Follow-Up Survey (TFS), "Current and Former Teacher Data Files," 2012–2013; *Teacher Attrition and Mobility Follow-Up Survey.* U.S. Department of Education, National Center for Education Statistics (NCES 2010–353)

are female between 1987 and 2012. Of particular interest is a slight decline in a White teaching force and a slight increase in a Hispanic teaching force.

A component of understanding the above trend is the attrition rate. Every year, teachers are leaving the profession for a variety of reasons; in order to understand who is in the field, we should understand whether there are trends among those leaving the profession. Figure 1.4 provides the percentage of movers and leavers. Apparent in this figure is the degree to which those moving within the field of education fluctuated between 1988 and 2013. Meanwhile, the percentage of individuals leaving the profession steadily rose during this timeframe. When analyzing this trend of movers and leavers by race/ethnicity, there is an apparent pattern of a slightly higher percentage of Black and Hispanic teachers leaving the profession compared to White teachers (see Figure 1.5). The implications of this trend are that given the limited presence of Black and Latino teachers, their elevated rate of leaving the profession raises questions as to whether the teaching workforce can be diversified without addressing the systemic issues outlined previously.

The integration project is also intimately connected to patterns of poverty. More specifically, as highlighted previously in the chapter, Black and Latino students are highly segregated by race and poverty status; in turn, so is the pattern of teacher allocation. Figures 1.6 and 1.7 demonstrate the percentage of teachers by race/ethnicity located in elementary and secondary schools serving student populations with more than 75% eligible for free and reduced lunch program (FRLP). Between 1999–2000 and

Figure 1.4   Percentage of Attrition Among Teachers in 1988–2013 SASS Survey

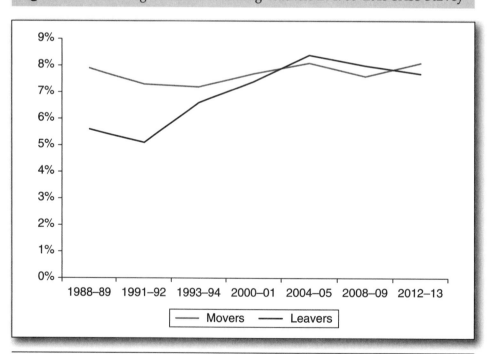

Source: U.S. Department of Education, National Center for Education Statistics, Teacher Follow-Up Survey (TFS), "Current and Former Teacher Data Files," 2012–2013; *Teacher Attrition and Mobility Follow-Up Survey.* U.S. Department of Education, National Center for Education Statistics (NCES 2010–353)

Figure 1.5   Percentage of Teacher Attrition: 2012–2013

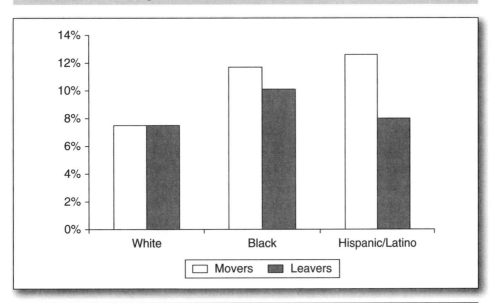

Source: U.S. Department of Education, National Center for Education Statistics, Teacher Follow-Up Survey (TFS), "Current and Former Teacher Data Files," 2012–2013; *Teacher Attrition and Mobility Follow-Up Survey.* U.S. Department of Education, National Center for Education Statistics (NCES 2010–353)

Figure 1.6   Percentage of Teacher Race/Ethnicity in Elementary Public Schools With 76%–100% of Student Population Eligible for Free and Reduced School Lunch

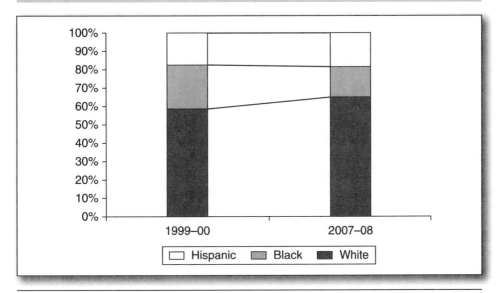

Source: U.S. Department of Education, National Center for Education Statistics, Teacher Follow-Up Survey (TFS), "Current and Former Teacher Data Files," 2012–2013; *Teacher Attrition and Mobility Follow-Up Survey.* U.S. Department of Education, National Center for Education Statistics (NCES 2010–353)

2007–2008 school years, the percentage of White teachers working in elementary schools with more than 75% of students eligible for FRLP increased from 56% to 62%. Simultaneously, the Black teacher percentage dropped from 23% to 16%, while the Latino teacher percentage barely

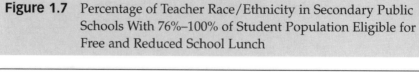

Figure 1.7   Percentage of Teacher Race/Ethnicity in Secondary Public Schools With 76%–100% of Student Population Eligible for Free and Reduced School Lunch

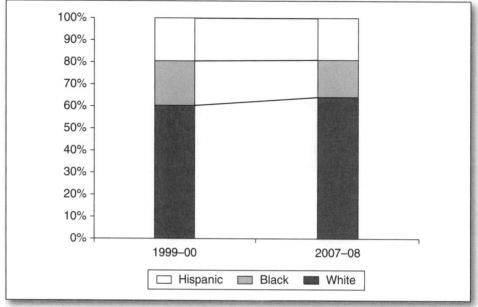

Source: U.S. Department of Education, National Center for Education Statistics, Teacher Follow-Up Survey (TFS), "Current and Former Teacher Data Files," 2012–2013; *Teacher Attrition and Mobility Follow-Up Survey.* U.S. Department of Education, National Center for Education Statistics (NCES 2010–353)

increased from 16.7% to 17.8%. A similar pattern is apparent in secondary schools. Between the 1999–2000 and 2007–2008 school years, the percentage of White teachers working in secondary schools with more than 75% of students eligible for FRLP increased from 58% to 61%. On the other hand, the Black teacher population dropped from 19% to 16%, and the Latino teacher population remained stable at 18%. The implications of this pattern are that as schools continue to become further hypersegregated by race and poverty status, White teachers are becoming the primary workforce in these schools. And as discussed earlier in the chapter, given the history of this country, every racial/ethnic group has limited intimate connections with persons from a different racial/ethnic group. This means that as White teachers are engaging with a growing racial/ethnic minority population, they maintain a limited scope of experience with populations different than them.

The conversation on principal presence is similar to that on teachers. The principalship is overwhelmingly White. Figures 1.8 and 1.9 provide the percentage of principals in elementary and secondary schools by race/ethnicity. At both school levels, Whites represent 80% of principals, and the 1999–2000 to 2007–2008 timeframe demonstrates this trend is stable.

When observing the principalship at schools with more than 75% of students eligible for FRLP, the patterns of integration are slightly different. Figures 1.10 and 1.11 demonstrate the percentage of principals by race/ethnicity in elementary and secondary schools with more than 75% of

Figure 1.8 Percentage of Principals by Race/Ethnicity in Elementary Public Schools

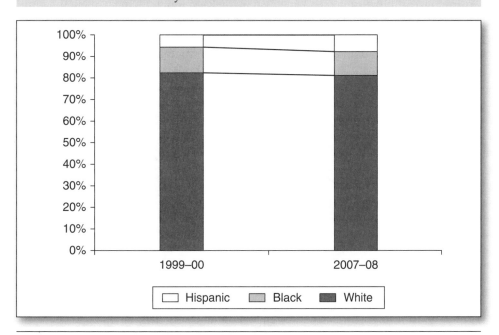

Source: U.S. Department of Education, National Center for Education Statistics, Teacher Follow-Up Survey (TFS), "Current and Former Teacher Data Files," 2012–2013; *Teacher Attrition and Mobility Follow-Up Survey.* U.S. Department of Education, National Center for Education Statistics (NCES 2010–353)

Figure 1.9 Percentage of Principals by Race/Ethnicity in Secondary Public Schools

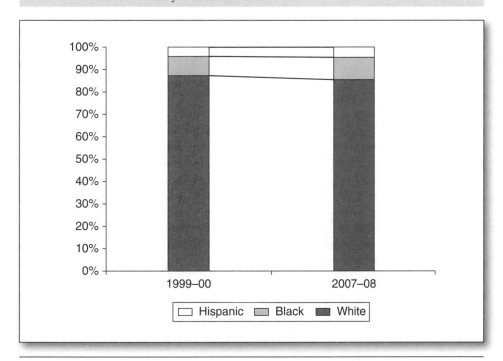

Source: U.S. Department of Education, National Center for Education Statistics, Teacher Follow-Up Survey (TFS), "Current and Former Teacher Data Files," 2012–2013; *Teacher Attrition and Mobility Follow-Up Survey.* U.S. Department of Education, National Center for Education Statistics (NCES 2010–353)

Figure 1.10 Percentage of Principal Race/Ethnicity in Elementary Public Schools With 76%–100% of Student Population Eligible for Free and Reduced School Lunch

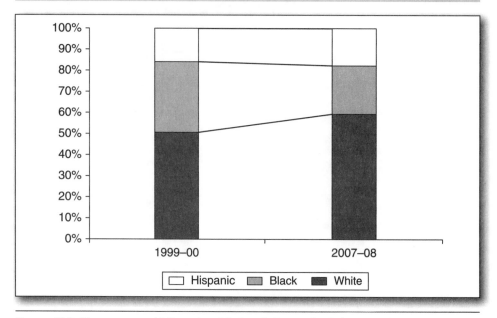

Source: U.S. Department of Education, National Center for Education Statistics, Teacher Follow-Up Survey (TFS), "Current and Former Teacher Data Files," 2012–2013; *Teacher Attrition and Mobility Follow-Up Survey.* U.S. Department of Education, National Center for Education Statistics (NCES 2010–353)

Figure 1.11 Percentage of Principal Race/Ethnicity in Secondary Public Schools With 76%–100% of Student Population Eligible for Free and Reduced School Lunch

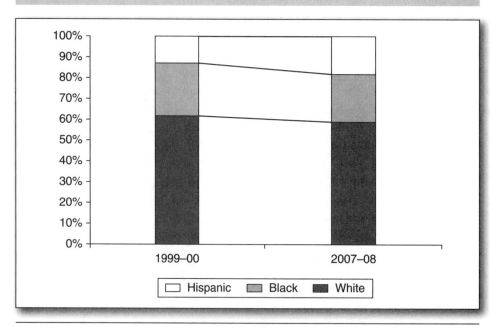

Source: U.S. Department of Education, National Center for Education Statistics, Teacher Follow-Up Survey (TFS), "Current and Former Teacher Data Files," 2012–2013; *Teacher Attrition and Mobility Follow-Up Survey.* U.S. Department of Education, National Center for Education Statistics (NCES 2010–353)

students eligible for FRLP. At the elementary level, during the 1999–2000 and 2007–2008 timeframe, Whites became the majority group represented in the principalship, 49% to 58% respectively, while the percentage of Black principals dropped from 33% to 22%, and the percentage of Latino principals grew slightly from 16% to 17%. At the secondary level, the integration project changed between 1999–2000 and 2007–2008. The percentage of White principals dropped slightly from 59% to 57%, and that of Black principals dropped slightly from 24% to 22%. However, the percentage of Latino principals grew the most, from 12% to 18%.

Overall, the demographics of the integration project are complex and require a variety of explorations and solutions. One of those areas of solution involves the development of teachers and principals that embrace equity as a core belief system for doing educational practice and policy. As I will discuss further in Chapter 2, I refer to equity that contains three components—numerical representation, social justice perspective, and culturally inclusive beliefs.

Another solution for this integration project is the diversification of the workforce. Although I consider the diversification of the teaching and leadership workforce to be a fundamental project that needs to continue, I do not consider the problem is centrally about too many Whites and women. Instead, the fundamental issue lies in the dominance of three types of bias-based beliefs—deficit thinking, colorblindness, and poverty disciplining. These beliefs thread through many aspects of educational policy and practice—from school discipline codes to special education referral processes, from the ways in which cognitive ability is defined and demonstrated to the ways in which we decide some schools need metal detectors and others not, to the ways in which some districts have schools with different entry criteria for gifted programs based on the rate of free/reduced lunch status. Our practitioner–student integration project is only a problem because our fundamental ethos of educational practice is dominated by deficit thinking, colorblindness, and poverty-disciplining bias beliefs. By beginning to address these dimensions of public and private belief systems, we have an opportunity to begin reconstructing school settings that behave like the moral compasses espoused in constitutions, state charters, religious deities, and local school vision statements. I truly believe that changing policies and practices cannot occur without ensuring that our public and private belief systems change along with it; otherwise, we are merely tinkering with the edges of change.

Chapter 2

Knowing the Bias-Based Beliefs in Disproportionality

We went through poverty training about 10 to 12 years ago, and one of the things that I remember from reading some of the books on poverty and the trainings is the need for us to understand that in Black culture they are loud, in Hispanic culture kids are not supposed to look at adults in the eye, and poor people have difficulty with time and use lots of humor to explain things. Will your trainings focus on some of these issues and how they impact their academic outcomes?

—High school principal (2015)

The research on cultural or implicit bias continuously makes the claim, "We all have biases." However, the challenge with biases is twofold: First, we need to recognize how they operate in implicit and explicit manners; and second, we have to replace them. In my own research on disproportionality, I am particularly interested in the nature of bias-based beliefs that set the stage for disproportionate referrals (Ahram & Fergus, 2011; Fergus, 2016), that is, educational beliefs that project ideas of cognitive and behavioral ability and capacity. The principal above articulates a bias-based belief about various cultural groups, that is, a belief that culture is static and that it helps in applying to school outcomes. His statement demonstrates how practitioners connect pedagogical concerns such as academic gaps with their own beliefs about culture as a static monolithic. As a school leader, his belief of Black culture as loud explains their school patterns of disproportionate suspension; the silent behaviors of Hispanic students explains their lack of engagement in the classroom; and low-income students' problems with time explain the issue of tardiness emerging among this group of students. Although we could argue that every individual maintains bias-based beliefs, the effects of these beliefs are dangerous when they are left unchecked and listed as reasons why all Black, Latino, or low-income kids are not attaining proficiency, are continuously getting a behavioral referral, or are not enrolled in gifted, talented, or honors/AP programs.

In this chapter, leaders are introduced to the bias-based beliefs that seep into pedagogy (i.e., the practice and method of teaching) and school practice (e.g., programs, team structures, and purpose, staffing arrangements). I focus on three bias-based beliefs—colorblindness, deficit thinking, and poverty disciplining. The exploration of these beliefs in this chapter is not only about defining them, but also about understanding as a leader how they operate within pedagogy and practice. Thus, I use Feldman and Pentland's (2003) notion of ostensive and performative components in organizational processes as a way of understanding how these bias-based beliefs operate in practice. Feldman and Pentland (2003) frame school processes as involving two components—the *ostensive component* (the ideal process) and the *performative component* (the actual process). As the terms allude, for every process, there is what we imagine it should be and how it will be executed (the ostensive), and then, there is the actual application of a process (the performative). These concepts help us to understand when bias-based beliefs can emerge. For example, during observations of Professional Learning Communities (PLC) throughout a school district with 10 schools, one elementary PLC team was reviewing a sample of student work, utilizing a protocol to guide them in their discussion. While looking at the outcome patterns of the student work, the team discovered that the students eligible for free/reduced lunch were achieving far below other students, and one teacher stated, "Come on, we need to understand that these kids are poor. It's hard for them to learn. The parents don't even show that they care about the college readiness stuff we send home!" Although PLC research has clearly established the differing mechanics of a good PLC (i.e., the ostensive component, or ideal), the performative component, as my example alludes, showcases how the presence of deficit thinking can derail an effective practice. We could also argue that the ostensive or ideal component of PLC was framed without the consideration of how a colorblind pedagogical lens can circumvent such a process. The challenge for leaders is to establish mechanisms in which to understand the dimensions of how bias-based beliefs appear in pedagogy, create opportunities to diminish such bias, and develop practitioner's self-efficacy (Fergus, 2016) and new equity principles that replace the need for these biases, thus encouraging healthy culture and climate for marginalized student populations (Fergus, Noguera, & Martin, 2014).

This chapter demonstrates what leaders need to understand about these forms of bias, and most importantly, it gives examples of how such biases present themselves throughout school environments. The examples are intended to provide school leaders with enough knowledge on the three bias-based beliefs so they are able to identify them. Furthermore, in Chapter 5, I provide activities to reduce these beliefs and minimize their malicious nature so they stop being a natural or normalized frame of the ostensive and performative components of school practice.

BIAS-BASED BELIEFS IN PEDAGOGY AND SCHOOL PRACTICE: HOW DOES IT SHOW UP IN SCHOOLS?

Substantive research highlights the relevance of bias, both implicit and explicit as operating in school settings. There are three types of bias-based beliefs relevant for leaders to understand: (1) colorblindness; (2) deficit thinking; and (3) poverty disciplining. We know from prior research that teacher ideologies and beliefs about the student population they serve can have a positive or negative effect on the student outcomes via the actions and behaviors teachers choose to employ in the classroom (e.g., Madon, Jussim, & Eccles, 1997; Madon et al., 1998; Madon et al., 2001; Proctor, 1984). Furthermore, in current research, bias-based beliefs in disproportionate school districts demonstrate colorblindness, racial discomfort, and deficit thinking as operating against teacher self-efficacy (Fergus, 2016). In other words, these bias-based beliefs are readily present when there is a lessened degree of teaching self-efficacy.

These beliefs, as I see them operating within the context of school policies and practices, are not mutually exclusive; they more often than not operate simultaneously. In fact, McKenzie and Scheurich (2004) claim that these beliefs are not only present in schools, but that leaders also struggle not knowing how to address them. The intention of this chapter is to equip school leaders with a complex understanding of these bias-based beliefs before moving forward onto how to structure staff and professional development in order for practitioners to replace those biases with equity principles.

COLORBLINDNESS BELIEF

I was working with a superintendent with whom I developed a great friendship. Let's call her Sally. During a fall opening conference day, I provided a keynote on different forms of bias. Specifically, I talked about colorblindness as a form of bias in which racial/ethnic minority groups that experience being racially identified by their skin color perceive colorblindness as an oversight of their social reality. On the other hand, Whites may perceive colorblindness as the act of not judging individuals based on skin color or other external markers. However, as I stated to the group, "Not seeing that I am a Black Latino male means that you are omitting the basis for some of my lived experiences." After the presentation, Sally approached me about her own confusion about colorblindness, "Eddie, I don't see your color and I don't treat you that way." And I responded candidly by saying, "If you are not seeing my color, that means you are treating me like yourself, which means that at some point I will do or say something that does not fit the image of the White woman you were treating me like." A colorblindness bias framework dangerously sustains a White cultural frame as the mode of looking at everything, such as when a White and Black student get into an argument in the hallway, or reprimanding Mexican American students for talking Spanish in the hallway, or continuously identifying Black students for "nice or matching clothes" they wear and not sufficiently for their good academic performance. In those examples, a White cultural frame omits the presence of different social realities due to identities that are different from a White social identity.

Eduardo Bonilla-Silva (2003) describes colorblindness as the new form of racial ideology that emerged after the civil rights era. Bonilla-Silva highlights the following as features of a colorblindness ideology: (1) the best form of removing racism is to omit race, gender, and other social identities as a descriptor; (2) it involves treating individuals as individuals and not considering their social identities; and (3) it focuses on discussing and framing the commonalities between individuals. Though viewing individuals' commonality is a desired state of humanity, colorblindness has also led to a pattern of rationalizing racial inequality as due to "market dynamics, naturally occurring phenomena, and Blacks' imputed cultural limitations" (p. 92). This ideology is used to make assertions such as, "Latinos' high poverty rate [due] to a relaxed work ethic, or residential segregation as due to natural tendencies among groups" (p. 92). A colorblindness belief views the presence of residential segregation in urban and suburban communities in connection to individual's home affordability and are blind to the subtle practices and processes of realtors limiting home or apartment views (Ondrich, 2003), or bank practices of subjectively rendering higher interest rates (Fishbein & Bunce, 2001) to low-income and racial/ethnic and linguistic minority groups. Colorblindness belief appears in explanations for differential outcomes in employment practices, even though numerous studies document patterns such as differential response to individuals based on race association to a name (Bertrand & Mullainathan, 2004), or Black applicants with no criminal record being offered low-wage jobs at lower rates than White applicants with a criminal record (Pager, Western, & Bonikowski, 2009).

A current example of colorblindness is the manner in which various charter schools and charter advocacy groups justify their arguments for school choice. Specifically, charter schools are framed as the optimal response to educational policies limiting pedagogical innovation. However, the charter school movement does not acknowledge that this absence of innovation stems from historical inequalities in the education of marginalized populations. In this case, failing to acknowledge such inequalities demonstrates a colorblind frame. Thus, a colorblindness belief prevents an individual from understanding how the historical, political, economic, and social translations of marginalized social identities into everyday practices is limiting access and opportunity, and thus create various reactions to limiting conditions (e.g., despair, anger, frustration, fear). It is these frames, as Bonilla-Silva describes, that operate as cul-de-sacs to interpret and rationalize the world; however, these frames misinterpret the world and make blind dominance and power in not having to ever experience or imagine marginalization.

Robin DiAngelo (2010, 2011) introduces two concepts critically important in supporting the continuation of colorblindness, making it a seductive intellectual and emotional and mental schema: (1) desire for individualism and (2) fragility of Whites in conversations beyond individualism. DiAngelo argues that Whites are enveloped by the experience and notion of being an individual; ways of seeing and traversing the world rests on an internal truth, "I am an individual. I make my own reality. I make my own path." However, this individualistic notion is erroneous according to the social science research on White–Black inequalities, which are primarily considered to be a result of social policies favoring Whites (Feagin, 2000). DiAngelo (2010) describes the manner in which individualism obscures experiences of marginalization:

> The Discourse of Individualism does more than posit that opportunity is equal and people arrive at their achievements through hard work alone, thus positioning dominant group members in a favorable light; it simultaneously obscures structural barriers and positions members of social groups who have achieved less in an unfavorable light. (pp. 4–5)

This discourse of individualism plays a prominent role in why practitioners will continuously focus on naming the racist act of the individual versus the systemic textures of racism based on 200 years of racialization. This "individualism" strategy for all intent removes racism as a systemic problem and assists in promoting the individual and colorblind perspective as a rational mental schema (see "Sample Colorblindness Statements"). In other words, as long as I understand racism as an individual act and not a system predicated on favoring certain characteristics and behaviors, I can feel absolved of any guilt and perceive the capacity of *not* seeing color as a more elevated social perspective.

DiAngelo's second concept, White fragility, speaks to the idea that when Whites encounter a slight level of racial stress due to their limited experience with racialized dialogue, they begin having emotional reactions like anger, guilt, blame, etc. Furthermore, DiAngelo (2011) argues that White fragility appears for several reasons: (1) Whites exist in segregated lives in which there are minimal feelings of loss when there are no

Sample Colorblindness Statements

I try to ignore skin color in order to view minority students as individuals.

Sometimes I wonder why we can't see each other as individuals instead of race always being an issue.

I try not to notice a child's race or skin color in the classroom setting.

Latino students who speak English should refrain from speaking Spanish at school so they don't alienate other students or teachers.

racially, ethnically, and linguistically diverse populations surrounding them; thus they have limited experiences to draw from to understand racism; (2) Whites' experiences of individualism obscure their perspectives to be understood as objective; and (3) Whites' perspective of themselves as outside of culture or "with no culture" encourages the idea of this experience as universal. Over time, colorblindness becomes treated and discussed as a more culturally evolved concept. It can be found among school practitioners who are continuously advocating, "Why can't we stop looking at each other based on color?" or "My students need to see their similarities, and not focus on differences." Thus, many teachers and administrators strive to build a colorblindness perspective among their students because they have a well-intentioned belief that, for example, if Black students successfully absorb the colorblindness perspective, this will be a cultural advancement for them, or if Spanish-speaking Latinos successfully adopt English language skills and remove Spanish language, it will be a cultural advancement for them.

What follows are various vignettes in which a colorblindness belief operated as a primer. The purpose of these vignettes is to provide an opportunity to practice understanding how the dimensions of a colorblindness belief appear in school settings. The incidents are based on actual events.

Vignette 1a: "I'm a good White person."

During a staff development observation, practitioners were sitting in circle discussing the latest book study, *Multiplication Is for White People* by Lisa Delpit, a book that challenges practitioners to consider the nuances that emerge in the lived experiences of Black students and what that means for educational practice. As the practitioners were sharing their thoughts, a White female elementary teacher shared the following:

> One of my African American students told me that her parents said that "White people can't be trusted, they discriminate against us." I told the student, "I care about you and that shouldn't apply to me; we need to like each other." It's things like that why we can't change parents.

How Is This Colorblindness Belief?

This teacher's understanding and response demonstrates several conditions prevalent in our school integration environments—(1) a desire to live colorblind and build that capacity among student, and (2) a preoccupation with not feeling or being guilty or at fault. School practitioners find themselves spewing the mantra of colorblindness to their students all the time: "It's not polite to describe each other by race"; "See each other's commonalities, not your race." The difficulty is that acknowledging an individual's social identities does not necessarily reduce them solely to that identity; in fact, it provides an opportunity to explore how social identities are historically, socially, economically, and politically constructed.

Vignette 2a: "I want answers in English only."

During a kindergarten field trip to the local zoo, the students along with the teacher were sitting in a training classroom with a zoo staff member. The White teacher asked the students to provide another word besides *big* to describe the animal the zoo staff member was holding. These 5- and 6-year-olds, which represented various ethnic groups, started using various foreign words, such as *grande* (Spanish), *grand* (French), and *groß* (German). The teacher immediately replied, "No, no. English only. I want your answers in English."

How Is This Colorblindness Belief?

The students in this example were actually demonstrating the beauty of cultural and linguistic diversity—the cultural variation in seeing the same thing. The practitioner in this situation could not see the asset in the students' cognitive capacities, but rather was blind to their diversity and centered the instruction around a "no-culture" approach.

Vignette 3a: "I don't see anything wrong with the Black students playing the role of slaves."

During a seventh-grade lesson on the Middle Passage, the slavery trade between west Africa and the Americas when Africans were boarded under inhumane conditions on overcrowded ships, a teacher wanted to help students understand the deplorable conditions experienced by Africans. The White teacher asked the only two Black female students in the class to bind their hands and feet and crawl under the desks in order to simulate the Middle Passage.

How Is This Colorblindness Belief?

In this example, the practitioner is blind to what it means to be the only Black students in a classroom and school, reducing students' Blackness to a performance, and in this curricular unit, forcing the Black students to perform a stereotypical notion of Blackness.

Vignette 4a: "I didn't mean anything by it . . . why didn't she say anything to me?"

This story was experienced by the author: Over the course of my daughter's third-grade school year, her hair became a point of concern. My daughter has really curly and big hair; her mother is a White Puerto Rican and I am a Black Panamanian. She started saying to us, "I want to straighten my hair so that nobody touches it," or "I hate my hair, I want it to be like everyone else's." We often talked about her wonderful hair. One day, she comes home and talks about not liking that sometimes her third-grade teacher would stand behind her while teaching a lesson and play with her hair! As concerned parents, we went and talked to the teacher about it, and we framed it that we want our daughter to feel culturally safe in the classroom. The teacher replied, "I didn't mean anything by it . . . why didn't she say anything to me?" And we replied that there is a power dynamic that will prevent kids from letting a teacher know that something he or she is doing is making them feel uncomfortable.

How Is This Colorblindness Belief?

This practitioner is allowing her individual fascination with curly hair drive her perception of why it is okay to touch someone else's hair. Her absence of experience in knowing what it is like to be part of social identity group in which hair is treated like an exotic artifact results in colorblind actions.

Vignette 5a: "But our school rules state that they have to say Mr. or Ms. when addressing a teacher. What's wrong with that?"

During a Spring semester working with a high school group on reducing the disparity in behavioral referrals and suspensions experienced among the Black and Latino students, a new school rule was instituted in which students needed to address all school staff as Mr. or Ms. After a quarter of implementing, the high school group noticed that Latino students were receiving an increased number of behavioral referrals for not following the new school rule. One committee member stated that the students are saying Maestra or Maestro (which is a formal way of addressing a teacher in various Latin American schools). However, the team struggled with whether they should allow them to say it in Spanish when the school rule states it must be Mr. or Ms.

How Is This Colorblindness Bias?

In this example, the practitioners are unable to understand how their rules reflect a colorblind perspective—that is, they did not take into consideration the 40% of Spanish-speaking Latino student population. Every policy and practice is developed from the premise of a universalized experience; the question for these practitioners and others is whether they are willing to redevelop those policies and practices once they are made aware of the colorblindness approach present, as well as their disproportionate outcomes.

Colorblindness Reflection Activity

The following reflection activity is intended to provide leaders an opportunity to practice the understanding of this belief. This practice involves being able to identify the types of social identities made invisible in each vignette and brainstorm the ways in which to address the issue in the moment or over time. Sometimes, the difficulty with addressing bias-based beliefs is "not knowing what to say"; this reflection activity helps to find an appropriate answer.

	What identities were made socially blind in this example?	Brainstorm strategies for addressing this situation.
Vignette 1a		
Vignette 2a		
Vignette 3a		
Vignette 4a		
Vignette 5a		

Copyright © 2017 by Corwin. All rights reserved. Reprinted from *Solving Disproportionality and Achieving Equity: A Leader's Guide to Using Data to Change Hearts and Minds* by Edward Fergus. Thousand Oaks, CA: Corwin, www.corwin.com. Reproduction authorized only for the local school site or nonprofit organization that has purchased this book.

DEFICIT-THINKING BELIEF

Richard Valencia (1997) defines deficit thinking as an ideology used within the field of education and in schools to explain academic performance as a result of deficiencies within an individual and group. A deficit ideology discounts the presence of systemic inequalities as the result of race-based processes, practices, and policies. Most importantly, a deficit ideology blames the group for the conditions they find themselves experiencing; as Valencia states, deficit thinking is "a type of cognition that is a relatively simple and efficient form of attributing the 'cause' of human behavior." According to Valencia, what supports this deficit thinking are three paradigms of thought: (1) genetic pathology model, (2) a culture of poverty model, and (3) a marginalization of low-income and students of color model. The first two models are of particular interest for describing the genesis and process of deficit thinking.

A genetic pathology model, popularized during the early 20th century, argued the "scientific" marking of hereditary or genetic traits (e.g., cranial size) was associated with "superior" genetic traits. The resulting theory was that individuals of European descent with better genetic traits were intellectually superior to individuals from other continents. The "science" of genetic pathology spurred the development of laws prohibiting interracial marriage in states such as California, Oklahoma, Maryland, and Louisiana, until these mandates became unconstitutional in 1967 (see *Loving v. Virginia*), as well as influenced the development of national legislative actions, such as the Immigration Act of 1924, which stipulated the restriction of individuals from specific countries (i.e., Southern and Eastern Europe). Although there is sufficient evidence to refute such genetic arguments, social remnants that support the idea of genetic differences between racial groups continue to surface (for example, cultural projects such as the PBS series "Finding Your Roots" and "African American Lives," which use forms of genetic testing to fuel the notion that race is biological and less about social construction).

Culture of poverty model, also known as cultural deficiency, refers to an explanation of poverty that argues the cultural attributes or practices often associated with historically disenfranchised racial/ethnic groups (specifically, Blacks and Latinos) have prevented them from assimilating and attaining social mobility within U.S. society. Examples of cultural deficiencies include limited attitudes and outlooks of the future, failure to internalize work value ethics, instant gratification behavior, lack of parent involvement in schools, low intellectual abilities, emphasis on masculinity and honor, and an aversion to honest work (see "Sample Deficit-Thinking Statements"). Other so-called deficiencies may include early initiation to sex

Sample Deficit-Thinking Statements

Students of color from disadvantaged homes just seem to show a lack of initiative.

Disadvantaged students generally do not have the abilities necessary to succeed in the classroom.

It is important that students of color assimilate so that they can succeed in mainstream American culture.

The values and beliefs shared by those in disadvantaged neighborhoods tend to go against school values and beliefs about what makes up a good education.

among children, female-headed households, fatalistic attitude toward life, and limited interest in education (Eitzen & Baca-Zinn, 1994). This notion seeks to establish a causal link between cultural attributes and socio-economic mobility.

The combination of these two concepts—genetic pathology and culture of poverty—provides the foundation for deficit-thinking bias. In other words, thinking of racial/ethnic minority groups as genetically inferior and culturally deficient supports deficit ideas of groups. Consider, for example, the deficit-thinking statements given above; each demonstrates how ideas of superiority and inferiority are projected upon and about racial/ethnic minority groups. Also, the vignettes that follow provide a closer look at the ways in which deficit thinking appears in some innocuous ways in our educational practice.

Vignette 1b: "Teachers need to see low-income communities."

When asked how he helps teachers understand where their student population comes from, a superintendent mentioned a bus tour organized for new teachers during the orientation week. New teachers are encouraged to participate in a bus tour going through the district and various communities. A particular emphasis, according to the superintendent, is on the low-income community. "I need for them to see where some of our Black and Latino students are coming from, and hopefully, they will have some sympathy."

How Is This Deficit-Thinking Belief?

Such types of "National Geographic" experiences with a singular focus on differences in neighborhoods, location, esthetics, etc., only reinforce the view of low-income environments as lacking resources. These tours do not include the framing of the resilient behaviors and accommodations found within low-income communities.

Vignette 2b: "Our kids' parents don't believe in education, especially college education."

During a school retreat focused on getting a staff of nearly 50 to agree on the values and beliefs about education, staff engaged in some fruitful conversation. While mapping the things that matter most to staff about education and the schooling process, several staff members shared out their idea on why parents are not on board: "Our kids' parents don't believe in education, especially college education." This sentiment was echoed by other staff members.

How Is This Deficit-Thinking Belief?

The deficit-thinking perspective is found in the interpretation of parental responses to college readiness as endemic of the problem. This type of interpretation is typical among individuals who pursued and obtained a college education and who believe that the process of attending college is universally understood and available for everyone.

Vignette 3b: "Immigrants don't belong in our community."

During a classroom observation of middle school English language arts, the teacher wanted to have the students practice the concept of compare-and-contrast using a Venn diagram. The teacher drew on the board a Venn diagram and then wrote "U.S. Citizen" in the left circle and "Illegal Immigrants" in the right circle. The students were then asked to describe the two groups. The following are the words offered by the students: "U.S. Citizen"—*belongs here, born here, speaks English, gets help from government, birth certificate,* and *nice neighbors*; "Illegal Immigrants"—*doesn't belong here, born in another country, speak Spanish and are loud, can't get help from the government, no papers, sometimes not nice neighbors,* and *your family helps you a lot.* After the students shared these perspectives, the teacher focused on practicing the compare-and-contrast skill.

How Is This Deficit Thinking Belief?

This example provides a nuanced operation of deficit thinking in which the practitioner does not need to espouse this belief, but rather creates the condition in which it shows up and by not redirecting the belief, the practitioner tacitly reinforces it. The deficit shown by the students is in the cultural inferiority of illegal immigrants: *not belonging here* and *being loud.*

Deficit-Thinking Reflection Activity

The following reflection activity is intended to provide leaders an opportunity to practice the understanding of this belief. This practice involves being able to identify the types of social identities framed as deficient in each vignette and brainstorming ways in which to address the issue in the moment or over time. Sometimes, the difficulty with addressing bias-based beliefs is the "not knowing what to say"; this reflection activity helps to find an appropriate answer.

	What identities were made socially deficient in this example?	Brainstorm strategies for addressing this situation.
Vignette 1b		
Vignette 2b		
Vignette 3b		

Copyright © 2017 by Corwin. All rights reserved. Reprinted from *Solving Disproportionality and Achieving Equity: A Leader's Guide to Using Data to Change Hearts and Minds* by Edward Fergus. Thousand Oaks, CA: Corwin, www.corwin.com. Reproduction authorized only for the local school site or nonprofit organization that has purchased this book.

POVERTY-DISCIPLINING BELIEF

This belief, similar to deficit thinking, points to low-income people as at fault for persistent adverse conditions; however, poverty-disciplining belief considers changing the behavioral and psychological dispositions of these individuals as paramount to fixing their low-income condition. In other words, deficit-thinking bias is focused on a set of beliefs about ability, while poverty-disciplining bias is focused on changing behavior and thinking of low-income individuals. Joe Soss, Richard Fording, and Sandford Schram (2011) frame in *Disciplining the Poor* that over the last 20 years social welfare policy has involved promoting the notion that low-income individuals "civic incorporation can be achieved only by forcing the poor to confront a more demanding and appropriate 'operational definition of citizenship'" (p. 5). In other words, in our society, we think and treat individuals living in low-income and extreme poverty conditions as requiring a level of disciplining so they could "learn the ways of being good citizens" and help themselves.

The practice that ensues from such a biased idea of individuals living in low-income conditions focuses on disciplining individuals into behaviors perceived as necessary/required for social mobility. For example, within the innovation of mixed-income housing (a housing strategy to integrate different income levels of families and individuals), various forms of disciplining the poor exist, and they are framed as "universal good resident" behaviors. For instance, since 2000, the Chicago Housing Authority has placed in mixed-income housing distinct restrictions on low-income renters and not for homeowners, such as renters cannot have grills on their patios, while homeowners can; renters cannot have visitors come and go freely; the building manager conducts "upkeep" visits of renters' units; and renters are required to attend classes on how to be a good neighbor. Another example of policy with a disciplining-the-poor bias involves the move by various state governments to limit the types of goods and services individuals living in low-income and extreme poverty are allowed to purchase with Temporary Assistance for Needy Families (TANF) dollars. In May 2015, the Kansas state legislature passed restrictions on the amount of money TANF recipients can withdraw from an ATM to $25 per day, which means less money they receive because each ATM withdrawal includes a user fee; additionally, TANF individuals are not permitted to redeem benefits at swimming pools, movie theaters, and tattoo parlors.

The last example of disciplining-the-poor bias can be found in the recent proliferation of "no excuses" approach to discipline in schools. The "no excuses" approach, most often associated with charter schools, but also prevalent in public schools, involves practices to change low-income and racial/ethnic minority student behaviors.

Sample Poverty-Disciplining Bias Statements

Poor people don't know the value of education and need to be educated about its value.

Poor kids are not exposed to the type of grit necessary to be successful in school.

Discipline is an important tool when working with poor kids.

They need to pull up their pants; otherwise they won't get jobs.

For example, in a charter network, students begin the school year on the floor and have to demonstrate appropriate behaviors in order "to earn" their desks, teachers, and other school activities; in several charter and public schools, students receive detention for dying their hair colors perceived as "unnatural" (e.g., pink, green, orange), wearing dangling earrings, or talking in the hallway between classes. In a large urban school district, the predominantly Black and Latino elementary schools require students to walk in the hallway pretending to have bubbles in their mouth and hugging themselves. This is called the "hugs and bubbles" approach.

A second component of this belief involves the premise that poverty causes compromised development among children and family units. O'Connor and Fernandez (2006) provide a succinct discussion arguing against this theory of compromised human development (TCHD). O'Connor and Fernandez list the following arguments: (1) poverty affects access to resources that influence child development; (2) the resource distribution only influences the effectiveness of the developmental process; (3) the reciprocal interactions between children, and parents are the engines that drive the developmental outcome; and (4) key interactions between child and parent such as verbal interactions, literacy tasks, disciplinary practices, and parenting approaches influence the developmental outcomes.

In the text box on page 42 are sample poverty-disciplining bias statements; each one reflects the notion of disciplining low-income individuals for being poor by changing their behavioral and psychological dispositions. Also the vignettes that follow provide a closer look at the ways in which poverty-disciplining bias appears in some innocuous ways in our educational practice.

Vignette 1c: "They need to pull up their pants . . . they just aren't serious about school and they won't get jobs like that."

During a walkthrough in a suburban high school, the principal was commenting on the "PBIS" signs posted throughout the hallway. At a point during the walkthrough, several Black boys walked by, and the principal turned to me and said, "Don't they know they need to pull up their pants . . . they just aren't serious about school and they won't get jobs."

How Is This Poverty Disciplining Belief?

The premise of the principal's statement is that this youth culture dressing style should be used as an example of school and work engagement. The principal is using an interpretive lens in which specific behaviors of low-income individuals need to be removed so that they would become successful. The reality is that all the behaviors and psychological dispositions of low-income individuals are perceived through the same lens—*their poverty is due to those individual behaviors, not the system.*

Vignette 2c: "We overly discipline our students because they are coming from poor conditions."

> During a district meeting about why they were being cited for disproportionate suspension of Black students, the superintendent began to argue the oversuspension of Black students is because they are poor, and not because they are Black. In fact, the superintendent conducted additional analysis to demonstrate this point: "See, these kids are poor, and do you understand how poor kids behave?"

How Is This Poverty-Disciplining Belief?

There is a common association between poverty status and the "culture of poverty" as demonstrative of behaviors opposite to the discipline code. Such perspective on what it means to live in poverty-laden conditions is biased due to several misconceptions: (1) There is a presumption that a discipline code provides a universal understanding of behavioral concepts, such as respect, obedience, etc.; (2) the behaviors associated with poverty status are stereotyped and portrayed as an antithesis to academic success and engagement; (3) disciplining children from poor conditions will minimize "poverty behavior" and enhance academic engagement; etc.

Vignette 3c: "Isn't the problem of disproportionality in special education because they are poor?"

> During a districtwide presentation on disproportionality with staff charged with providing interventions, a school psychologist posed a question that many practitioners explicitly state or implicitly suggest: "Have you looked at this data by poverty? Because isn't the problem of disproportionality in special education because they are poor?" My response focused on describing the research that discounts the significance of poverty as a contributor.

How Is This Poverty-Disciplining Belief?

There is a sentiment that poverty obstructs development of children from low-income families, and high classification rates in special education represent a rational response to this fact. Furthermore, the role of special education is to accommodate or discipline such children for having a compromised human development. This misguided notion treats the markers of disability categories as objective and does not consider that they are influenced by subjective views of evaluation practitioners.

Poverty-Disciplining Reflection Activity

The following reflection activity is intended to provide leaders an opportunity to practice the understanding of this belief. This practice involves being able to identify the types of behaviors that need to be changed in each social identity and brainstorming ways in which to address the issue in the moment or over time. Sometimes, the difficulty with addressing bias-based beliefs is the "not knowing what to say"; this reflection activity helps to find an appropriate answer.

	What identities involved poverty disciplining in this example?	Brainstorm strategies for addressing this situation.
Vignette 1c		
Vignette 2c		
Vignette 3c		

Copyright © 2017 by Corwin. All rights reserved. Reprinted from *Solving Disproportionality and Achieving Equity: A Leader's Guide to Using Data to Change Hearts and Minds* by Edward Fergus. Thousand Oaks, CA: Corwin, www.corwin.com. Reproduction authorized only for the local school site or nonprofit organization that has purchased this book.

Chapter 3

Leadership Inquiry Skills for Building Equity Focus

I n this chapter, I present the critical tasks school and district leaders need to work on to ensure that equity-driven beliefs become embedded in the fabric and ethos of a school, district, and hopefully, community. More specifically, this chapter focuses on the mechanics of data (see Appendix 1 for a Data Inventory Worksheet), data systems, and data teams in driving whether and how shifting the beliefs of practitioners alongside systemic policy and practice implementation is determining the outcome. The chapter is organized into two sections: (1) understanding your data and data system capacity; and (2) practicing understanding of disproportionality patterns by analysis and interpretation of data.

SECTION 1: UNDERSTANDING YOUR DATA AND DATA SYSTEM CAPACITY

As an applied researcher who provides consultant support on equity system reform and specifically on utilization of data and data matrices, I often hear from school and district leaders, "How should I look at the data?"; "When should I look at them?"; or "I'm looking at data but am not sure what they are telling me." Some of these questions have to do with a skill capacity—*do I have data and research analysis skills*—and they also have to do with an interpretation capacity—*what is this telling me, and how do I connect it to practice and policy?* This section provides some clear pathways for school and district leaders to build these two capacities as they embark on examining disproportionality and its related bias-based beliefs. Many of the exercises can and should be conducted with a leadership inquiry or equity team.

Data and Research Analysis Capacity: Measuring Your Readiness to Use Data

Research on leaders' use of data points to a myriad of realities. For example, principals and district administrators construct data into different formats (Park, Daly, & Guerra, 2012), while the types of district- and school-level conditions determine how the data are used (Datnow, Park, & Wohlstetter, 2007), and other conversations have a singular focus on data utilization as part of accountability rather than school improvement (Jennings, 2012; Marsh, 2012). Although all are necessary dialogues regarding data and their use, my intention in this section is to focus on basic skills of leaders, such as knowledge of data systems, knowledge of data, and data-usage culture focused on improving conditions.

What you will find on the following pages are several forms to be completed by administrators. The questions are intended to be self-assessment; thus, it's imperative that you think carefully about your answers. At the end of each self-assessment question section is an opportunity to reflect on your answers, and more importantly, what to do next to make self-improvements. In considering your self-improvement plans, identify what skills you need for tomorrow, next semester, and next year.

To prepare for the proceeding exercises, make sure to compile the following information necessary for each self-assessment activity:

Activity 1: Software Competency. Collect the names of various data software available across the district and school.

Activity 2: Assessment Competency. Collect the names of the various assessments available across the district and school.

Activity 3: Data Analysis Competency. No preparation necessary.

Activity 4: Infrastructure Competency. Collect the names of the team meetings and their use of data.

Activity 1: Software Competency

*The purpose of these questions is to explore **your** capacity and competency with the various forms of software available in your district. Insert the names of the software systems used in your district in the blank spaces.*

1. What's your level of comfort with the following software?

	Highly Comfortable	Somewhat Comfortable	Not Comfortable at All	Unfamiliar With Software
Excel	○	○	○	○
SPSS	○	○	○	○
_____	○	○	○	○
_____	○	○	○	○
_____	○	○	○	○
_____	○	○	○	○

2. How often do you use the following software as part of your leadership role?

	Everyday	Two or Three Times a Week	Once Every Other Week	Once a Month	At the End of Marking Period	Never
Excel	○	○	○	○	○	○
SPSS	○	○	○	○	○	○
_____	○	○	○	○	○	○
_____	○	○	○	○	○	○
_____	○	○	○	○	○	○
_____	○	○	○	○	○	○

Identify Next Steps for Improvement *(Consider using the software developers' training series, especially if they have an online component; consider identifying at least two other staff members to learn software utilization—it's easier to practice with a partner than alone):*

_____

_____

_____

Copyright © 2017 by Corwin. All rights reserved. Reprinted from *Solving Disproportionality and Achieving Equity: A Leader's Guide to Using Data to Change Hearts and Minds* by Edward Fergus. Thousand Oaks, CA: Corwin, www.corwin.com. Reproduction authorized only for the local school site or nonprofit organization that has purchased this book.

Activity 2: Assessment Competency

The purpose of these questions is to explore **your** *capacity and competency with the various forms of assessment available in your district. Insert the names of the various assessments conducted with your children.*

1. What's your level of comfort with the following assessments?

	Highly Comfortable	Somewhat Comfortable	Not Comfortable at All	Unfamiliar With Assessment
_____	○	○	○	○
_____	○	○	○	○
_____	○	○	○	○
_____	○	○	○	○
_____	○	○	○	○

2. How often do you look at the following assessment as part of your leadership role?

	Everyday	Two or Three Times a Week	Once Every Other Week	Once a Month	At the End of Marking Period	Never
_____	○	○	○	○	○	○
_____	○	○	○	○	○	○
_____	○	○	○	○	○	○
_____	○	○	○	○	○	○
_____	○	○	○	○	○	○

Identify Next Steps for Improvement *(Consider using the assessment developers' training series, especially if they have an online component; consider identifying at least two other staff members to learn assessment utilization—it's easier to practice manipulating data with a partner than alone; make sure to understand the optimal assessment conditions and purpose of assessment):*

_____

_____

_____

_____

Copyright © 2017 by Corwin. All rights reserved. Reprinted from *Solving Disproportionality and Achieving Equity: A Leader's Guide to Using Data to Change Hearts and Minds* by Edward Fergus. Thousand Oaks, CA: Corwin, www.corwin.com. Reproduction authorized only for the local school site or nonprofit organization that has purchased this book.

Activity 3: Data Analysis Competency

*The purpose of these questions is to explore **your** capacity and competency with conducting analyses.*

1. What are the questions you consider important to examining attendance data?

_____

_____

_____

_____

_____

_____

_____

2. What are the questions you consider important to examining behavior/discipline data?

_____

_____

_____

_____

_____

_____

_____

3. What are the questions you consider important to examining achievement data?

_____

_____

_____

_____

_____

_____

_____

(Continued)

(Continued)

4. What are the types of data that you look at on a daily, monthly, quarterly, and annual basis?

Daily	Monthly	Quarterly	Annually

Copyright © 2017 by Corwin. All rights reserved. Reprinted from *Solving Disproportionality and Achieving Equity: A Leader's Guide to Using Data to Change Hearts and Minds* by Edward Fergus. Thousand Oaks, CA: Corwin, www.corwin.com. Reproduction authorized only for the local school site or nonprofit organization that has purchased this book.

Activity 4: Infrastructure Competency

The purpose of these questions is to explore **your** *capacity and competency to establish structures that use data to drive improvements.*

1. List any teams in your building that use data (e.g., professional learning communities, intervention teams, grade level teams, content teams).

Name of Team	Frequency of Team Meetings	Data Used

2. Name types of data teams listed above use within their meetings:

	Yes or No	If yes, provide the name of data source (e.g., Wonders curriculum benchmark).	List the years of data implementation.
Diagnostic data			
Benchmark data			

Identify Next Steps for Improvement (*Depending on your answers above, consider defining how to extend the data usage capacity of your various infrastructures; consider including these teams as part of improvement activities named in Activities 1–3):*

_____

_____

_____

_____

_____

_____

Copyright © 2017 by Corwin. All rights reserved. Reprinted from *Solving Disproportionality and Achieving Equity: A Leader's Guide to Using Data to Change Hearts and Minds* by Edward Fergus. Thousand Oaks, CA: Corwin, www.corwin.com. Reproduction authorized only for the local school site or nonprofit organization that has purchased this book.

Critical Reflection

1. What do you now know about your capacity and your systems capacity?

_____

_____

_____

_____

_____

_____

2. What are the areas of competency and capacity promise? Competency and capacity challenge?

_____

_____

_____

_____

_____

_____

3. What are the overall activities that need to take place over the next 3, 6, and 12 months? And what are the related resources necessary for these activities to occur?

Data Capacity Needed	Steps Necessary to Achieve Capacity	Timeframe Range

Closing Reflection

The toughest part of conducting a self-assessment is not the assessment itself, but not being inhibited by the thought that "there is so much to do." Question 3 of Critical Reflection is intended to make leaders focus on small segments of the overall goal.

SECTION 2: PRACTICING ANALYSIS AND INTERPRETATION OF DATA: CASE STUDIES

In this section, I provide six case studies to assist leaders in practicing applying their equity-driven principles, in addition to some basic steps of looking at data. Furthermore, the case studies encourage the focus to be on numerical, social justice, and cultural and beliefs-oriented goals.

Case Study 1: Recognizing Discipline Patterns

The data presented in Table 3.1 provide a snapshot of discipline patterns with several points of *longitudinal* information. The information is given within a high school context with nearly 1,200 students and the following racial/ethnic structure: 48% White, 30% Black, 9% Hispanic, 8% Asian, and 5% Other. Review Table 3.1 and identify the types of patterns present in the example. Before jumping to conclusion and solutions (i.e., "Based on this, I think the problem is . . ."), an equity-driven leadership team must have a clear understanding of the problem; you can't fix something based on superficial or gut feelings.

Table 3.1   Discipline Referrals

	1	2	3	4	5	6	7	8	9
A	SY	April R.	Total R.	April Black R.	Total Black R.	% Black R. in April	% Black R. Total	R. Gap	% Non-Black R.
B	2011	324	2402	225	1777	69%	74%	48%	26%
C	2012	118	1801	84	1171	71%	65%	30%	35%
D	2013	117	1017	69	744	59%	73%	46%	27%
E	2014	176	1076	82	806	47%	75%	50%	25%

Key: R = Referrals; SY = School Year.

Case Study Direct Instruction Moment: What should I see?

NOTE: A number and letter combination will be used to indicate a specific cell in the table; for example, (6,B) refers to column 6 and row B.

1. The number of referrals in April across the various school years decreased; however, a more important decrease is in the proportion of Black student referrals. In 2011, Black referrals accounted for 69.4% (6, B) of the monthly total, and in 2014, the number was down to 47% (6, E).

2. Although for April the number of Black student referrals decreased between 2011 and 2014, the percentage of Black student referrals did not change. In 2011, Black students accounted for 74% of all referrals (7,B), and in 2014, they accounted for 75% (7,E), which means no changes in the referral gap. In other words, the referral gap between Black students and all other students is 48% (8,B) in 2011 and 50% (8,E) in 2014. This gap is obtained by subtracting the percentage of non-Black referrals (9,A) from the percentage of total Black referrals (7,A).

Case Study Equity Questions

1. What are some processes, practices, and policy areas to be examined?

_____

_____

_____

_____

_____

_____

2. What are some social justice–oriented concerns about these patterns?

_____

_____

_____

_____

_____

_____

Case Study 2: Suspensions Live in Referrals

The data presented in Tables 3.2 and 3.3 provide a snapshot of discipline patterns with several points of *longitudinal* information. The information is given within a high school context with nearly 1,500 students and the following racial/ethnic structure: 45% White, 34% Black, 9% Asian, 7% Hispanic/Latino, and 5% Other.

Table 3.2 Suspension Data

	1	2	3	4
A		2011–2012	2012–2013	2013–2014
B	All Students	229	159	155
C	White	39	35	29
D	Black	168	102	106
E	Multiracial	9	7	6
F	Latino	12	13	9
G	Asian	1	2	2
H	SWD	43	32	43
I	FRLP	190	129	127
J	% of suspensions Black	73%	64%	68%
K	% of suspensions non-Black	27%	36%	32%
L	% of suspensions White	17%	22%	19%

Table 3.3 Behavioral Referral Data

	1	2	3	4
A		2011–2012	2012–2013	2013–2014
B	All Students	1804	1152	1076
C	White	442	268	166
D	Black	1171	755	806
E	Multiracial	73	50	37
F	Latino	100	55	55
G	Asian	18	19	12
H	SWD	285	185	222
I	FRLP	1420	935	909
J	% of referrals Black	65%	65%	75%
K	% of referrals non-Black	35%	35%	25%
L	% of referrals White	25%	23%	15%

Case Study Direct Instruction
Moment: **What should I see?**

NOTE: A number and letter combination will be used to indicate a specific cell in the table. For example, (6,B) refers to column 6 and row B.

1. In Table 3.2, there is an apparent drop in the rate of suspensions between 2011 (2,B) and 2014 (4,B). However, the drop is not evenly experienced across the various racial and ethnic groups. In fact, Black students had a greater decline between 2011 (2,J) and 2014 (4,J), compared to White students between 2011 (2,L) and 2014 (4,L).

2. In Table 3.3, there is an apparent drop in the rate of behavioral referrals between 2011 (2,B) and 2014 (4,B). However, the drop is not evenly experienced across the various racial and ethnic groups. In fact, Black students had an increase in their percentage representation rate between 2011 (2,J) and 2014 (4,J), compared to White students in 2011 (2,L) to 2014 (4,L). Also, the decline experienced between 2011 (2,B) and 2014 (4,B) is mainly due to the decline among White students between 2011 (2,L) and 2014 (4,L).

3. Comparing Tables 3.2 and 3.3 to the overall school composition of 45% White, 34% Black, 9% Asian, 7% Hispanic, and 5% Other demonstrates a classic disproportionate representation. For example, among overall suspensions (Table 3.2), Black students represented 73% in 2011 (2,J) and 68% in 2014 (4,J) of suspensions, while they make up approximately 30% of the enrolled student population; this is a classic example of overrepresentation.

Case Study Equity Questions

1. What are some processes, practices, and policy areas to be examined?

_____

_____

_____

_____

_____

_____

2. What are some social justice–oriented concerns about these patterns?

_____

_____

_____

_____

_____

_____

Case Study 3: Not as Equally Gifted

Tables 3.4 and 3.5 list various points of analysis with regard to gifted program enrollment at the elementary level. The information is derived from a school district with over 40,000 students and the following racial/ethnic elementary-level enrollment: 44% White, 30% Latino, 13% Asian, 8% Black, and 5% Other.

Case Study Direct Instruction Moment: What should I see?

NOTE: _A number and letter combination will be used to indicate a specific cell in the table. For example, (6,B) refers to column 6 and row B._

1. In Table 3.4, there is an apparent pattern of White (6,B) and Asian (3,B) students comprising the largest proportion of the gifted program enrollment. However, this distribution is not proportional with the district enrollment. In fact, Latino students comprise 30% (5,C) of elementary-age student enrollment, yet only 17% (5,B) of gifted program enrollment.

2. The apparent pattern is the composition rate (1,D) among all groups. Among Asian students, 21% (3,D) are enrolled in gifted programs at the elementary level compared to their White peers enrolled at only 8% (6,D); however, their rate is higher than Black students, 2.3% (4,D), and Latino students, 4.7% (5,D).

3. The next apparent pattern is the _relative risk ratio_ (1,E). According to these data, Asian students are over 3 times more likely to be in gifted programs compared to Black students (4,E) and Latinos (5,E).

Table 3.4 Gifted Composition in Elementary Schools

	1	2	3	4	5	6	7	8	9
A		Native American	Asian	Black	Latino	White	Pacific Islander	Multiracial	Total
B	Composition of students enrolled in gifted program	0.1%	32.4%	2.4%	17%	42.7%	0.1%	5.3%	100%
C	Composition of students enrolled in district (K–5 only)	0.4%	12.8%	8.3%	30.1%	43.9%	0.2%	4.3%	100%
D	Composition of group in gifted programs (within group risk index)	1.1%	21%	2.3%	4.7%	8%	4.6%	10.4%	8.3%
E	Relative risk ratio	0.14	3.28	0.27	0.48	0.95	0	1.27	

Table 3.5 AP/Honors Composition in High Schools

	1	2	3	4	5	6	7	8	9
A		Native American	Asian	Black	Latino	White	Pacific Islander	Multiracial	Total
B	Students enrolled in gifted program	0.3%	29.7%	3.3%	11.9%	50.5%	0.1%	4.3%	100%
C	Students enrolled in district (Grades 9–12 only)	0.5%	11.6%	9.9%	28.5%	45.6%	0.2%	3.7%	100%
D	Composition of group in gifted programs (within group risk index)	4.6%	24%	3%	4%	10.5%	4%	11%	9.4%
E	Relative risk ratio	0.49	3.23	0.30	0.34	1.22	0	1.15	

Case Study Direct Instruction
Moment: What should I see?

NOTE: A number and letter combination will be used to indicate a specific cell in the table. For example, (6,B) refers to column 6 and row B.

1. In Table 3.5, there is an apparent pattern of White (6,B) and Asian (3,B) students comprising the largest proportion of the gifted program enrollment. However, this distribution is not proportional in district enrollment. In fact, Latino students comprise 29% (5,C) of elementary-level enrollment, yet only 12% (5,B) of AP/honors program enrollment.

2. The apparent pattern is the composition rate (1,D) among all groups. Among Asian students, 24% (3,D) are enrolled in gifted programs at the high school level compared to their White peers with only 11% (6,D); however, this rate is higher than for Black students 3% (4,D) and Latino students 4% (5,D).

3. The next apparent pattern is the *relative risk ratio* (1,E). According to data, Asian students are over 3 times more likely to be enrolled in gifted programs compared to Black students (4,E) and Latinos (5,E).

Case Study Equity Questions

1. What are some processes, practices, and policy areas to be examined?

_____

_____

_____

_____

_____

_____

2. What are some social justice–oriented concerns about these patterns?

_____

_____

_____

_____

_____

_____

Case Study 4: Fixing Academic Referrals Leading to Special Education Classification

In Table 3.6, various points of analysis are provided regarding special education referrals and classification at the district level. The information is derived from a school district of over 8,000 students with the following racial/ethnic student enrollment: 89% White, 6% Black, 3% Hispanic, 1% Asian, and 1% Other.

Table 3.6 Referral to Special Education Classification Rates

	1	2	3	4	5	6
A		Black	Hispanic	White	Asian	Total
B	Number referred to intervention services	20	11	119	3	153
C	Total enrolled	520	284	7336	87	8227
D	Percentage of referrals	3.85%	3.87%	1.62%	3.44%	1.85%
E	Number recommended to special education	20	8	102	3	133
F	Percentage of referred recommended	100%	72%	85%	100%	87%

Case Study Direct Instruction Moment: What should I see?

NOTE: A number and letter combination will be used to indicate a specific cell in the table. For example, (6,B) refers to column 6 and row B.

1. Table 3.6 provides referral and recommendation numbers for a school district during a school year. Overall, the district refers a small percentage, 1.85% (6,D), of the overall student population for an additional intervention support. However, when you look within each racial/ethnic group, only White students' referral rate, 1.62% (4,D), is comparable to the district rate (6,D). Meanwhile, Black (2,D), Hispanic (3,D), and Asian (5, D) students maintain higher referral rates.

2. The rates of referral to special education are high across all groups. Among the Black student population referred to intervention support, 100% (2,F) are recommended for special education services; similar are the high rates among Hispanic students (3,F), White students (4,F), and Asian students (5,F).

Case Study Equity Questions

1. What are some processes, practices, and policy areas to be examined?

_____

_____

_____

_____

_____

2. What are some social justice–oriented concerns about these patterns?

_____

_____

_____

_____

_____

Case Study 5: High Special Education Classification Doesn't Happen Overnight

In Table 3.7, various points of analysis are provided regarding special education classification at the district level. The information is derived from a school district of over 10,000 students with the following racial/ethnic student enrollment: 73% White, 18% Asian, 6% Latino, and 3% Black.

Table 3.7 Special Education Classification

	1	2	3	4
A		2008–2009	2009–2010	2010–2011
B	District enrollment of SWD	15%	15%	16%
C	Black SWD	54%	51%	46%
D	White SWD	15%	15%	20%
E	Latino SWD	26%	27%	3%
F	Asian SWD	2%	2%	2%
G	Relative risk ratio of Black students	3.98	3.67	3.06

Case Study Direct Instruction
Moment: What should I see?

NOTE: A number and letter combination will be used to indicate a specific cell in the table. For example, (6,B) refers to column 6 and row B.

1. In Table 3.7, the overall district enrollment of students with disabilities (SWD) is consistent over 3 school years—(2,B); (3,B); and (4,B). In addition, the rate of Black students shows a downward trend over the 3 school years. However, the rate of Black students receiving special education services points to severe disproportionality; specifically, in 2008–2009, more than 1 in every 2 (2,C) Black students was receiving special education services. On the other hand, White students maintained the rate of 15% in 2008 (2,D) and 2009 (3,D).

2. Another pattern resulting from these rates of classification is the *relative risk ratio*. Black students in this school district were 4 times more likely than all other students to receive special education services in 2008 (2,G) and 3 times more likely in 2010 (4,G).

Case Study Equity Questions

1. What are some processes, practices, and policy areas to be examine?

_____

_____

_____

_____

_____

_____

2. What are some social justice–oriented concerns about these patterns?

_____

_____

_____

_____

_____

_____

Case Study 6: Reading About Your Identity During Adolescence

A significant conversation point in culturally responsive pedagogy and instruction (Gay, 2000, 2002; Ladson-Billings, 1994) is the relevance of seeing oneself within the cultural milieu of curriculum, both hidden and explicit, as well as instructional engagement. This case study involves the novels used in an English language arts curriculum developed by a district curriculum team, and it reviews how seeing oneself can be explored within a task as simple as reading popular classic fiction. The core equity question explored is whether the protagonists and antagonists portrayed in these novels reflect the district population. In addition, the question is whether these novels reflect a broader global context of diversity. Tables 3.8, 3.9, and 3.10 list the novels, the percentage of district enrollment by race, and the percentage of books whose protagonists are of the same race/ethnicity as the student population.

Case Study Direct Instruction Moment: What should I see?

NOTE: A number and letter combination will be used to direct you to a specific cell in the table. For example, (6,B) refers to column 6 and row B.

1. In Tables 3.8–3.10, Whites are most often represented as the protagonists in the novels for students Grades 6 through 12. This means that other racial and/or ethnic groups are either not present or that they appear in an antagonist role.

2. A Black character appears only in one book, *Mississippi Trial 1955*, a historical novel plotted around the murder of Emmitt Till. According to curriculum, students in this district are never introduced to this Black protagonist.

Table 3.8 Sixth-Grade English Curriculum Novels

Novels	Demographic	Percentage of District Student Enrollment	Percentage of Books With the Protagonist of the Same Race/Ethnicity
Maniac Magee, Jerry Spinelli	White	65%	50% (3 out of 6 books)
Breadwinner, Deborah Ellis	Black	15%	0%
A Family Apart, Joan Lowery Nixon	Latino	16%	0%
Perloo the Bold, Avi*	Asian	4%	0%
Crispin the Cross of Lead, Avi	Middle Eastern or North African	0%	33% (2 out of 6 books)
A Place in the Sun, Jill Rubalcaba			

*Main character is an animal.

Table 3.9   Eighth-Grade English Curriculum Novels

Novels	Demographic	Percentage of District Student Enrollment	Percentage of Books With the Protagonist of the Same Race/Ethnicity
Tunes for Bears to Dance To, Robert Cormier	White	65%	75% (6 out of 8 books)
Mississippi Trial, 1955, Chris Crowe	Black	15%	0%
Choosing Up Sides, John Ritter	Latino	16%	0%
Beowulf, Robert Nye	Asian	4%	0%
The Wave, Todd Strasser	Middle Eastern or North African	0%	0%
Animal Farm, George Orwell*			
The Call of the Wild, Jack London*			
The Diary of Anne Frank			

*Main character is an animal.

Table 3.10   Eleventh-Grade English Curriculum Novels

Novels	Demographic	Percentage of District Student Enrollment	Percentage of Books With the Protagonist of the Same Race/Ethnicity
A Time to Kill, John Grisham	White	65%	85% (6 out of 7 books)
The Crucible, Arthur Miller	Black	15%	0%
The Great Gatsby, F. Scott Fitzgerald	Latino	16%	15% (1 out of 7 books)
Othello, William Shakespeare	Asian	4%	0%
The Old Man and the Sea, Ernest Hemingway	Middle Eastern or North African	0%	0%
The Sun Also Rises, Ernest Hemingway			
The Scarlet Letter, Nathaniel Hawthorne			

Case Study Equity Questions

1. What are some processes, practices, and policy areas to be examined?

_____

_____

_____

_____

_____

_____

2. What are some social justice–oriented concerns about these patterns?

_____

_____

_____

_____

_____

_____

Chapter 4

A Process for Identifying Disproportionality and Building an Equity Plan

For years, teachers, principals, and district administrators would tell me, "Show us how to do the data, what to look at, and when!" More often than not, I would do so; however, there was an underlying principle that affected how I looked at data, how I used them, and when I used them. This principle was equity. My pedagogical vision was framed by equity—how can we ensure that students who need more support receive it in an appropriate manner? Are the systems optimized to work for the most vulnerable, those who are also known as school-dependent kids? How are social identities such as race, gender, disability, etc. treated as different? How can close examination of school systems allow leaders to minimize the effect of bias-based beliefs? These are some of the questions built into my equity lens.

As discussed in previous chapters, the utilization of data serves as only one of various tools necessary to attain equity. The other tools include an understanding of bias-based beliefs among practitioners, activities that sustain the replacement of these beliefs, and activities for developing a shared school climate equity vision. As I work with schools and districts, I remind them that this work does not take "extra" time. In fact, these activities can be done in professional learning communities (PLCs), grade-level or content meetings, shared planning time, and so on.

This chapter is organized into four steps: (1) identifying the need for a root cause analysis; (2) root cause process for identifying disproportionality problems; (3) monitoring equity work; and (4) progress-monitoring tools. As a way of deciding where to start as a school/district leader, Figure 4.1 illustrates a decision tree for school and district leaders to define where and how to begin. The decision tree is built on a particular premise and follows a sequence of work (see Sample Road Map) to assist school and/or district leadership in plan implementation.

STEP 1: IDENTIFYING YOUR STARTING PLACE

Name your last root cause analysis (RCA): *Has your school or district conducted a root cause analysis in the last 2–3 years?*

- There are multiple questions to begin a journey with a school or district, but a consistent and paramount question I always ask is about the type and frequency of prior analyses on equity concerns: *Has your school or district conducted a root cause analysis in the last 2–3 years?* The answers to this question allow understanding on different levels: If the answer is yes, then what was the reception, process, outcome, implemented change, and inevitably, why am I here? If the answer is no, then I ask why not, what is the interest for these conversations, and what are the underlying problems to consider when beginning this journey. Understanding the history of exploring equity concerns in a school community is a relevant lever of implementation and change that needs to be considered in any endeavor on this topic.

Yes, **our district or school has conducted a root cause analysis in the last 2–3 years.**

- The presumption I make here is that this analysis included close examination of outcome and process data. At times, district or school leadership share with me that they conducted the "five *why*'s" process for their root cause analysis, which in its most generic form involves looking at outcome data and asking five *why* questions, and it will lead to root causes. As an efficient and generic process, it is fraught with opportunities for subjective and biased answers to each *why* question. Make sure the root cause analysis is robust.
- If a robust RCA has been conducted, then create an updated summary of the RCA and share it with school/district members in a professional development setting. This sequence of work can occur during Year 1 Months 2–3.
  - While the summary is being rolled out, the school or district leadership team should conduct Chapter 5 Stage 1 activities as a team to practice the sequence of the activities, the potential reactions, and their own comfortability with leading these belief conversations. This sequence of work can occur during Year 1 Months 2–3.

- Create and implement a professional development plan using the Planning Sheet for Addressing Beliefs and Building Equity Principles (see Appendix 2). The Exit Ticket form (see Appendix 3) can be filled after each activity with staff to gauge reception, understanding, and belief growth. This sequence of work can occur during Year 1 Months 4–7.

● Utilize the progress-monitoring tools in this chapter. This sequence of work can occur during Year 1 Months 1–9.

Figure 4.1 Disproportionality Decision Tree

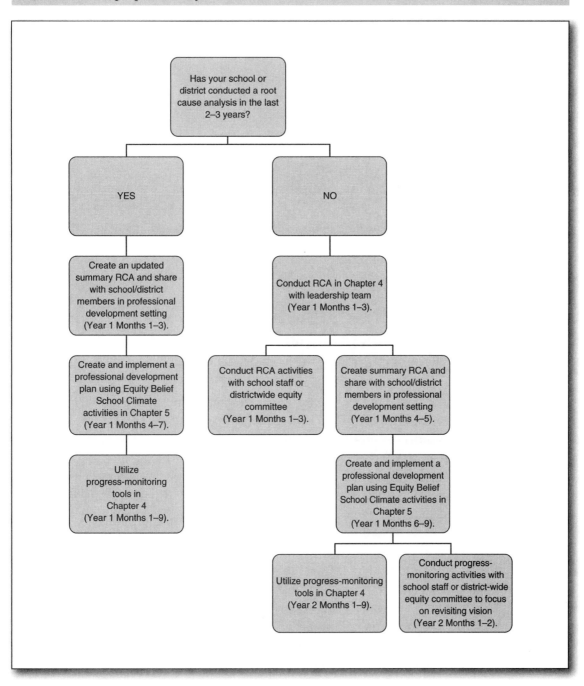

No, **our district or school has not conducted a root cause analysis in the last 2–3 years.**

- This chapter contains a detailed outline of conducting a robust RCA on special education classification and referral, behavioral referrals and suspension, and gifted, AP, honors, or accelerated programs. This process focuses on examining outcome and process data. This sequence of work can occur during Year 1 Months 1–3.
- Once the RCA has been conducted, create a summary of the RCA findings and share with school/district members in a professional development setting. The Exit Ticket form can be filled with staff to make sure that the current state of disproportionality is clear. This sequence of the work can occur during Year 1 Months 4–5.

  - While the summary is being rolled-out, the school or district leadership team should conduct Chapter 5 Stage 1 activities as a team to practice the sequence of the activities, the potential reactions, and their own comfortability with leading these conversations. This sequence of the work can occur during Year 1 Months 4–5.
  - Create and implement a professional development plan using the Planning Sheet for Addressing Beliefs and Building Equity Principles (see Appendix 2) activities in Chapter 5. The Exit Ticket form (see Appendix 3) can be filled after each activity with staff to gauge reception, understanding, and belief growth. This sequence of the work can occur during Year 1 Months 6–9.

- Utilize the progress-monitoring tools in this chapter. This sequence of the work can occur during Year 2 Months 1–9.

STEP 2: ROOT CAUSE PROCESS FOR UNDERSTANDING DISPROPORTIONALITY PROBLEMS

A framework I use to name and understand disproportionality problems is root cause analysis (RCA). In generic terms, RCA refers to a data- and research-driven process for naming the causes of disproportionate patterns (see Figure 4.2). For example, an RCA approach to examining an achievement gap between White and Latino students would consider the magnitude of the performance gap (i.e., specific achievement differences in scale scores, course grades, content area, curricular strands), timing of practices (i.e., specific achievement differences in the magnitude compared by quarters, semesters, and school years), location of practices (i.e., specific achievement differences in the magnitude by classrooms and grade levels), and policy and practice conditions (i.e., specific achievement differences in the magnitude by pre- and postinterventions, pre- and postcurriculum change implementation, fidelity of intervention, and curricular implementation).

An RCA process involves quantitative and qualitative data. More often than not, an RCA process reveals the systematic nature of how practice and

Figure 4.2 Root Cause Analysis—Overview of Levels

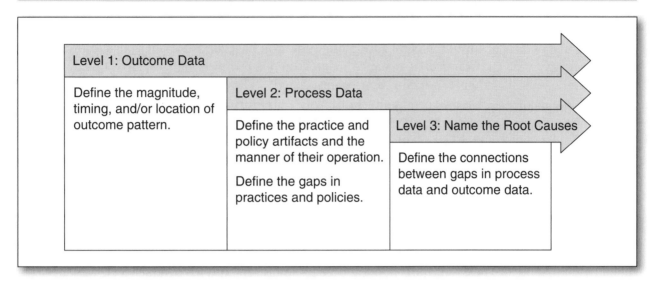

policy gaps can allow the presence of bias-based beliefs about marginalized populations to operate as a "rationale" for disproportionate patterns (Ahram & Fergus, 2011). As I discussed in Chapter 2, bias-based beliefs about cognitive and behavioral ability and habits are viewed as actual pedagogical rationales for why some kids do better than others. For example, whenever I present data on racial/ethnic disproportionality in special education classification to a group of practitioners, inevitable are the following bias-based questions about the cognitive ability: "But have you looked at these data by poverty status? Don't you think this happens because students come from poverty conditions?" The distorted logic behind such questions is that individuals living or growing up in poor conditions are surrounded by limited words, limited print-rich environments, inconsistent adult supervision, the absence of concerted cultivation parenting, and presence of natural growth parenting (Lareau, 2003) and that unhealthy adult relationships *create* a disability (National Research Council, 2002). This bias-based belief also known as compromised human development (O'Connor & Fernandez, 2006) treats the cognitive and behavioral ability of children from low-income environments as normed against the child development of children from middle-class environments and with a race-neutral approach. The scope of this bias-based belief can be detected in the thinking processes of how practitioners recommend children for academic interventions based on perceptions of student effort, how interventionists understand a diversity in literacy schemas of children who use an oral language for literacy development, and how principals understand student behavioral responses in school climates that are not culturally safe for racial/ethnic minority students. Thus an RCA process (see Figure 4.2) does not only detect practice and policy gaps and how bias-based beliefs operate in these practices and policies, but it also targets remedies while leaders change the pedagogical beliefs that get in the way of effective school environments.

Common Root Causes: Findings From a 10-Year Data-Driven RCA Process

From 2004 to 2013, I served as the director and co-principal investigator of the New York State Center on Disproportionality (also known as the Technical Assistance Center on Disproportionality [TACD]—www.stein hardt.nyu.edu/metrocenter/tacd). During this time, I developed the Disproportionality Root Cause Analysis process. TACD's work involved assisting school districts cited for disproportionality to (1) understand the citation; (2) identify the root causes of this outcome; (3) develop a strategic plan for addressing the root causes; and (4) implement the plan and develop capacity to continuously monitor rates of disproportionality. Over the course of developing and piloting a data-driven process (2004–2010) for identifying root causes, I gained insight into not only the root causes, but also the driving forces (internal and external to district) of these root causes. This data-driven root cause process focused on examining various areas of the schooling process to understand the interaction of school practice (inputs) and student outcomes. This process involved examining the following three areas: *quality of curricular and instructional supports* (e.g., type of core program, stage of core program implementation, capacity of instructional staff, and learning outcomes of students), *intervention services for struggling students* (e.g., type of available interventions, frequency of intervention usage, stage of implementation, length of intervention implementation, and number of students participating in intervention programs by race/ethnicity, gender, and grade level), and *predominant cultural beliefs* (perceptions of race and class, perceptions of different learning styles versus a disability, perceptions of how race and class interact in school practice, and cultural responsiveness of current policies and practices).

The examination of these data in countless districts has resulted in identification of common disproportionality root causes. These causes are not the only ones, but they tend to be present in every district and maintain the most significant effect on the rate of disproportionality in school districts. An important trend to note about these root causes is the manner in which they appeared in districts. More specifically, the policy and practice causes appeared as either *misalignments* or *absent* from the school reform. For example, in one district cited for the overrepresentation of Black students in special education, the district decided to change the threshold of a kindergarten readiness screener and raise it 25% higher than recommended by the developer. As an elementary principal stated, "The majority of our students are high performing, so we needed to change the benchmark." Over time, such change resulted in 56% of the Black student population being identified with a disability. This type of action is an example of misalignment—the execution of a practice and/or policy is not aligned with its intended purpose, but is instead aligned with a bias-based belief. A common example of absent policy and/or practice involves school discipline. More often than not, codes of conduct are based on punishment and not on research according to which responses to misbehavior should focus on the function of the behavior, not the behavior itself. This type of action is an example of absent programs/policy—the lack of specific practice, program, or policy based on limited knowledge of shifting needs.

Cause 1: Gaps in Curriculum and Instructional Implementation Disproportionately Affect Struggling Learners

Endemic in most school districts is the question of instructional wellness that includes responsiveness—does and can our instruction maximize the learning capacity of all students? In our data-driven root cause process, multiple causes emerged as contributing to disproportionality rates. The wellness of instruction and curriculum as it is represented in instructional support teams/teacher assistance teams, intervention services, assessment, and gifted and talented programs continuously emerged as maintaining gaps in practices that disproportionately affected struggling learners.

1. **Minimally articulated core curriculum and consistent support of teaching ability.** Due to various factors, many school districts did not have in place a *current* curriculum and/or agreement on instructional approaches that would be appropriate for a wide-range of learners. As a result, students that persistently could not attain proficiency on the state exam were promptly considered for special education services. Additionally, some districts were continuously changing or adding curriculum, assessment, and instructional strategies from year to year. Although every school district contends with such changes, we found in our districts such structural changes affected struggling learners the most. For example, practitioners tended to comment that they lacked the ability to adequately service students at the lowest quartile of performance. Therefore, instructional staff go through a steep learning curve regarding a new curriculum and/or assessment, feeling inadequate to address skill deficiencies with students, even based on the prior curricula or assessment.

   The policy change in IDEA 2004 regarding response to intervention (RTI) has greatly encouraged the conversation among practitioners to recognize the impact of an inadequate curriculum, particularly in reading, for struggling learners. Many school districts are acknowledging the absence of a reading series and program as preventing them from truly understanding and locating the reading capacity of students in Grades K–5.

   Remedy: Identification and sustained implementation of appropriate reading and math core program that is sequenced K–12. Additionally, sequenced and sustained support for nontenured and tenured teaching staff to build ability to effectively implement curriculum and/or assessment, as well as instructional capacity.

2. **Too many interventions for struggling learners.** In examination of curriculum and the related interventions, we found that many school districts maintained an exhaustive list of interventions for

students demonstrating academic difficulty. The overabundance of interventions for struggling learners meant the core curriculum as an intervention and the related instructional capacity of staff was not organized to address the needs of a range of learners. Unfortunately, without a well-articulated core curriculum and instructional program that services all students, this gap disproportionately affected not only struggling learners, but also new students to the districts (including newly arrived English Language Learners).

Remedy: Identification and implementation of targeted intervention programs (i.e., research-based) for students demonstrating academic difficulty while core curriculum program is re-developed.

3. **Inconsistent knowledge of the purpose and implementation of assessments.** Various school districts were utilizing assessment tools developed to screen students at risk for reading difficulty as the measures of diagnosing reading skill deficiency. However, there was inconsistent knowledge about these assessments, that is, what information do they capture, how can you translate the assessment information into targeted interventions, etc. For example, some school districts were utilizing assessment tools developed to merely screen students at-risk for reading difficulty to diagnose reading skill deficiency. In another district, the kindergarten screening being used maintained a specific threshold of what students are potentially at risk, and the common practice with this assessment was to go 25% above that threshold and identify all those students as "not ready" for their school environment. This inconsistent knowledge base regarding assessments allowed for interventions and strategies not tailored for meeting the specific needs of struggling learners. Therefore, instructional support teams and/or child study teams would receive information about a child's reading difficulty sometimes after months or a year of inadequate interventions.

Remedy: Continuous professional development on purpose, application and interpretation of curriculum, assessment and instructional strategies.

4. **Adding behavioral intervention services without addressing school climate.** Some of the patterns that emerged in the root cause included schools and at times districts adding behavioral intervention services to "fix" problem behaviors and limited identification of how climate contributed to behaviors. For example, one school district decided to provide one-on-one behavioral aides for "problem" kids which resulted in walking into any school and seeing mostly Black boys being shadowed by college-age White or Asian males. Such practices emerge from a focus of addressing an urgent issue but not identifying the causal factors or function of the factor and the ways in which the environment may contribute to the problem behavior.

Remedy: Determine interventions and school climate conditions that address the function of student behavior and improve climate toward engagement.

5. **Intervention services for struggling learners are not well structured.** The root cause process revealed the implementation of interventions programs was inconsistent and became the gateway for special education referrals. For example, students referred and classified tended to reach below basic proficiency over multiple school years. Meanwhile, the academic intervention staff did not receive training on moving students from below basic proficiency into proficiency; they tended to receive training focused on moving students that would assist a school in reaching Adequate Yearly Progress (AYP), which are generally those students just below proficiency. The long-term effect is twofold: (1) students who are far below proficiency are not given the adequate and sustained opportunity to accelerate their learning; and (2) students who are barely into proficiency tend to "slide" in and out of proficiency; thus, they are constantly receiving instruction and interventions that are only enough to get them to proficiency, but not enough to master academic skills.

    Remedy: Redevelopment of a tiered system of academic supports for struggling learners, identification of research-based interventions for targeted groups of students, and targeted professional development for academic intervention staff (i.e., nontenured and tenured, including content specialists).

Cause 2: Inconsistent Prereferral Process

1. **Inconsistency in referral process, including referral forms.** School districts are generally good at ensuring they abide by special education regulations, including referral timeframes, involvement of practitioners, etc. However, the RCA process also found school districts maintained inconsistent prereferral information, as well as different forms for each school building in a district. Again, much of these system inconsistencies were not intentional, but rather reflective of the bifurcation existing in the district between special education and general education. In many instances, special education directors would describe how they could only suggest to building administrators adopting one common referral form or insisting on general education teachers to complete the specifics of the prereferral strategies.

    Remedy: Development of a common process and form for prereferral and outline annual process for examining the wellness of this process. Provide training on appropriate interventions and fidelity of implementation for general education teachers.

2. **Limited information regarding intervention strategies.** One of the steps in the root cause process is to conduct a records review of a

representative sample of files; this ranged from 40 to 100 files, depending on the number of students receiving special education services. On most forms, the RCA process found a text box in which general education teachers would describe the strategies they previously tried. In most instances, general education teachers annotated how moving a student's seat, matching them with a buddy, or providing the content or skill again, but at a slower pace, did not work, even though they considered it a viable strategy. The plethora of strategies lacked any sense of viability as a competent strategy and also lacked any sense of summative evaluation as to its impact. Teachers tended not to note any type of pre-/postevaluative summary; instead, the standard answer was "I tried and it didn't work." Even with the addition of RTI in IDEA 2004, which requires school districts to revamp their prereferral/problem-solving team forms such that they request information about interventions provided by general education teachers, there still is a gap in knowledge among practitioners regarding what is and is not an intervention in Tier 1.

Remedy: Provide training on evidence-based interventions and fidelity of implementation for general education teachers and instructional support teams/teacher assistance teams.

Cause 3: Limited Beliefs of Ability

1. **Special education is viewed as fixing struggling students.** In most school districts, the general and special education staff rarely interact with each other. The RCA process brought together cross-district teams that included general and special education teachers, administrators, content specialists, etc., and more often than not conversation was interrupted due to a limited understanding among practitioners regarding what is a disability. General education teachers tended to express the belief that special education maintains the "magic fairy dust" that will "fix" the learning capacity and outcomes of students. Some of this belief may be due to the reality that prior to the addition of RTI in IDEA 2004, the special education process was perceived as organized to provide services to students outside of the normal curve of academic performance. Though RTI is part of conversation in most school districts, some practitioners viewed RTI as the new process for "getting student classified" and not a process for ensuring quality instruction and interventions.

Remedy: General and special education participate in professional development regarding curriculum, assessment, and instructional strategies together, including special education regulations; analysis of data regarding interventions for struggling students must involve general and special education teachers.

2. **Poor and racial/ethnic minority students are viewed as not "ready" for school.** During Equity Belief School Climate sessions (Chapter 5), school and/or district staff shared that somehow being

poor/low-income and being from a racial/ethnic minority group compromises how "ready" these students are for their school environment (Ahram & Fergus, 2011). More specifically, school and district staff perceived at times the cultural practices of the home environment as making low-income and racial/ethnic minority children unable to learn, or contradicting school practices. For example, in one district, many of the participants rallied around the concept of "urban behavior" as a driving force of why the Black students were in special education. In another district, English Language Learners were overrepresented in special education with speech/language impairment because in "Latin culture, they listen to music loud"; this was hypothesized by an ESL teacher. And yet another district hypothesized the Latino and ELL students are such a distraction in the classroom that they can be better served with other disability groups. Such perspectives are not solely found in school districts cited for racial/ethnic disproportionality anymore; in fact, such perspectives can be found in many urban, suburban, and rural districts as well. Part of the difficulty with such a belief is its distraction from engaging how teaching matters in learning outcomes. That is, the belief sessions found practitioners were willing to cite the family and community (i.e., poverty, limited reading materials at home) as the reason why poor/low-income and racial/ethnic minority students were struggling academically, while attributing the academic performance of proficient students to their teaching practice. So there needs to be a paradigm alignment regarding the connection between teaching and learning, as well as an understanding of how to harness the types of knowledge students demonstrate.

Additionally, these predominant beliefs regarding poor/low-income and racial/ethnic minority students as "different" also resulted in students feeling a sense of stereotype threat and vulnerability because their low-income or racial/ethnic minority status as a "risk" factor. For example, in several districts, focus groups were with students to ascertain what it took to get good grades; low-income and racial/ethnic minority students often cited feeling seen and treated as different.

Remedy: Continuous professional development on creating culturally responsive school environments with particular sessions on stereotype threat, vulnerability, racial/ethnic identity development within the five developmental domains, examination of whiteness (Apple, 1997; Blanchett, 2006; Cooper, 2003), and cultural developmental expressions as additive not subtractive (Irvine & York, 2001; Ladson-Billings, 1999).

To embark on a process of remedying your district or school of disproportionate representation, it must begin with a substantive inquiry into why and how these patterns exist.

Overall, the disproportionate representation of racial/ethnic minority and low-income students in special education, discipline, and gifted programs is a complex occurrence that requires a deliberate inquiry process, which seriously considers practices and policies as having to be responsive to the population of students served, regardless of ability and demographics.

Starting the RCA Process: Forming a Disproportionality Leadership Team

The RCA process should be undertaken by a leadership team. The leadership teams could vary in size from 5 to 20 members depending on whether it is an RCA of a school, a set of schools, or a school district. The following are potential members that could be included in the leadership team:

- Superintendent (or representative, i.e., Assistant Superintendent, Pupil Services Director)
- Building Leadership: K–12
- General Education and Special Education Teachers (elementary, middle, and high school)
- Program Leadership: ESL, title programs, special education, guidance and counseling, etc.
- Representatives from intervention and special education review committees
- Representatives of Board and union leadership
- Parent(s) and/or local parent groups
- Local college or university faculty
- Local agencies or community groups that provide support to the school, district, and/or students who are disproportionately represented in special education, discipline, and gifted programs

Overview of Disproportionality Data Tools

This section is intended to guide schools or school districts through a basic analysis of their gifted/AP/honors, special education, and discipline outcome data, as well as their academic and behavioral referral and intervention policies and practices. This requires a review of quantitative data as well as qualitative review of practices and processes. These RCAs are designed to provide a rigorous analysis of disproportionality. The bias-based beliefs in practices and policies simultaneously are designed to help schools and districts engage in conversations about disproportionality and equity.

The quantitative data primarily relies on three main data tools (calculations): risk index, composition index, and relative risk ratio. Because of the relative strengths and weaknesses of each tool, it is best to use as many of the tools as possible at a given level. While each tool can give some information, using all three tools will create a more complete statistical picture.

The *composition index* gives the proportion of students by race/ethnicity in a particular situation. Composition indexes are used to determine if a particular group is over- or underrepresented in special education, in a particular disability, or in a suspension infraction category, behavioral referral, and gifted/AP/honors programs.

The *risk index* identifies what rate, or percentage of risk, students have of having a particular outcome—e.g., classification as a student with disability, discipline referral, suspension. This measure can be applied to an entire population of students or a particular group of students—e.g., student groups by race and ethnicity, gender, socioeconomic status.

The *relative risk ratio* gives a comparison of risk for classification of one group in relation to the risk for all other groups. A risk ratio of 1.0 indicates that there is equal risk. A risk ratio above 1.0 is indicative of increased risk. A risk below 1.0 indicates a decreased risk. For example, a risk ratio of 1.5 for Black students translates to Black students are 1.5 times more likely than other groups to experience a specific outcome.

Data Needs for Root Cause Analysis

As we all are aware, data take many forms in educational practice. Data can be found in attendance records, classroom observation notes, running records, state exam results, behavioral referrals, department meeting notes, climate surveys, etc. Now that the leader and/or leadership team has defined a focus, a subset of inquiry areas (Chapter 3), it is important to identify the forms of data that will be helpful in answering those questions. A first step in this part of the process is connecting the form of data the inquiry team considers most useful for helping to answer your inquiry. Exercise 1 with your leadership team should take about 20 minutes.

To assist leadership teams in building an outline of the types of data that could be explored regarding various inquiry foci pertinent to disproportionality in special education and academic referrals, behavioral referrals and suspensions, and gifted/AP/honors program enrollment, I provide an aggregate look at the myriad data specific to these inquiry areas in Exercise 2. These charts are not exhaustive, but they can provide a landscape from which a leadership team can begin conducting a focused inquiry cycle on disproportionality.

Exercise 1: Data Inventory for Inquiry

Inquiry Number	Description of Data	Reason for Data Collection	Who will collect these data, and when?

Copyright © 2017 by Corwin. All rights reserved. Reprinted from *Solving Disproportionality and Achieving Equity: A Leader's Guide to Using Data to Change Hearts and Minds* by Edward Fergus. Thousand Oaks, CA: Corwin, www.corwin.com. Reproduction authorized only for the local school site or nonprofit organization that has purchased this book.

Exercise 2: Sample Data Inventory

Discipline and Behavioral Referrals: *What should you be collecting/gathering?*

Inquiry Focus	Description of Data	Reason for Data Collection	Analysis Questions
Discipline referrals	A representative sample of discipline records by building, race, gender, incident type, and response to incident	Analyze patterns in the reason for referrals by race and gender, and the response by incident type.	Are Black students being referred for different disciplinary reasons compared to White students?
Discipline policy (building and district level)	School and district conduct manuals	Analyze school/district discipline policies.	Are discipline policies clearly defined? How are students and staff made aware of discipline policies? How are expected behavioral norms taught?
Disciplinary practices	Sample discipline referral form	Examine the type of information collected on the form, and discuss how the form is used.	What information is gathered? How do these forms shape the discipline process?
	Sample behavior plans	Examine the quality of the behavior plans.	Do the plans use research based strategies? How well are the plans implemented?
	Interventions List	Examine the types of available behavioral interventions.	Do the interventions focus on replacement strategies? Is there a plan for implementation and support (e.g., FBA, BIP)?

Gifted/AP/Honors Program: *What should you be collecting/gathering?*

Inquiry Focus	Description of Data	Reason for Data Collection	Analysis Questions
Gifted/AP/honors enrollment	A representative sample of gifted/AP/honors records by building, race, and gender.	Analyze patterns in the enrollment of gifted/AP/honors by race and gender, and grade level.	Are Black students being enrolled in gifted/AP/honors programs compared to White students?
Gifted/AP/honors program enrollment policy (building and district level)	School and district program enrollment manuals	Analyze school/district program enrollment policies.	Are gifted/AP/honors program process policies clearly defined? How are staff made aware of gifted/AP/honors program process policies?
Gifted/AP/honors program practices	Sample gifted/AP/honors program referral form	Examine the type of information collected on the form, and discuss how the form is used.	What information is gathered? How do these forms shape the referral process?
	Sample gifted/AP/honors program plans (e.g., curriculum, lesson plans)	Examine the quality of the program plans.	Do the plans use research based strategies? Is the program focused on "more work" or advanced work?

Special Education and Academic Referrals: *What should you be collecting/gathering?*

Inquiry Focus	Description of Data	Reason for Data Collection	Analysis Questions
Special education classifications	A representative sample of special education records by building, race, gender, disability types	Analyze patterns in the disability types by race and gender, and grade level.	Are Black students being referred for different disability types compared to White students?
Academic referral policy (building and district level)	School and district academic referral manuals	Analyze school/district academic referral policies.	Are academic referral process policies clearly defined? How are staff made aware of academic referral process policies?
Academic referral practices	Sample academic referral form	Examine the type of information collected on the form, and discuss how the form is used.	What information is gathered? How do these forms shape the referral process?
	Sample intervention plans	Examine the quality of the intervention plans.	Do the plans use research based strategies? How well are the plans implemented?
	Interventions List	Examine the types of available academic interventions. (*Note:* Focus on one content area, preferably reading/literacy.)	Do the interventions focus on remediation and/or acceleration strategies? Is there a plan for implementation and support of interventions?

Root Cause Analysis 1: Disproportionality in Special Education Classification

The 2004 IDEA reauthorization outlined State Performance Plan (SPP) includes a focus on disproportionality in special education; SPP Indicator 9 looks at representation of culturally and linguistically diverse students in special education relative to all other students; SPP Indicator 10A looks at representation of culturally and linguistically diverse students in specific disability categories relative to all other students. This initial look at your school's or district's special education referral and classification data is meant to provide both a framework to examine equity in special education outcomes and to help your team pose questions about your school's or district's academic referral and intervention policies and practices.

Level 1 Analysis: Outcome Data

Using your school's data, complete the following tables and answer the reflection questions.

Enrollment

1. How many students are enrolled in your school or school district?

	American Indian or Alaskan Native	Asian or Pacific Islander	Black or African American	Hispanic or Latino	White	Multiracial	Total
Student Enrollment	A	B	C	D	E	F	G

2. What is the composition of your school or school district?

	American Indian or Alaskan Native	Asian or Pacific Islander	Black or African American	Hispanic or Latino	White	Multiracial	Total
Student Enrollment	$A \div G \times 100 =$	$B \div G \times 100 =$	$C \div G \times 100 =$	$D \div G \times 100 =$	$E \div G \times 100 =$	$F \div G \times 100 =$	100%

All Students With Disabilities (SWD)

3. How many students with disabilities are enrolled?

	American Indian or Alaskan Native	Asian or Pacific Islander	Black or African American	Hispanic or Latino	White	Multiracial	Total
Students With Disabilities (All Categories)	A	B	C	D	E	F	G

4. What is the composition of the students with disabilities?

	American Indian or Alaskan Native	Asian or Pacific Islander	Black or African American	Hispanic or Latino	White	Multiracial	Total
Students With Disabilities (All Categories)	A ÷ G × 100 =	B ÷ G × 100 =	C ÷ G × 100 =	D ÷ G × 100 =	E ÷ G × 100 =	F ÷ G × 100 =	100%

5. What is the risk index (classification rate) of students from each racial/ethnic group being classified as students with disabilities? What are the relative risks of students from each racial/ethnic group being classified as students with disabilities compared to all other students?

	American Indian or Alaskan Native	Asian or Pacific Islander	Black or African American	Hispanic or Latino	White	Multiracial	Total
Student Enrollment	A	B	C	D	E	F	G
Students With Disabilities (All Categories)	H	I	J	K	L	M	N
Risk Index	H ÷ A × 100 =	I ÷ B × 100 =	J ÷ C × 100 =	K ÷ D × 100 =	L ÷ E × 100 =	M ÷ F × 100 =	N ÷ G × 100 =
Relative Risk	(H ÷ A) ÷ [(N – H) ÷ (G – A)] =	(I ÷ B) ÷ [(N – Q) ÷ (G – B)] =	(J ÷ C) ÷ [(N – J) ÷ (G – C)] =	(K ÷ D) ÷ [(N – K) ÷ (G – D)] =	(L ÷ E) ÷ [(N –L) ÷ (G – E)] =	(M ÷ F) ÷ [(N – M) ÷ (G – F)] =	

Students Classified With an Emotional Disturbance (ED)

6. How many students are classified with an *Emotional Disturbance (ED)*?

	American Indian or Alaskan Native	Asian or Pacific Islander	Black or African American	Hispanic or Latino	White	Multiracial	Total
Emotional Disturbance (ED)	A	B	C	D	E	F	G

7. What is the composition of the students classified with an *Emotional Disturbance (ED)*?

	American Indian or Alaskan Native	Asian or Pacific Islander	Black or African American	Hispanic or Latino	White	Multiracial	Total
Emotional Disturbance (ED)	A ÷ G × 100 =	B ÷ G × 100 =	C ÷ G × 100 =	D ÷ G × 100 =	E ÷ G × 100 =	F ÷ G × 100 =	100%

8. What is the risk index (classification rate) of students from each racial/ethnic group being classified with an *Emotional Disturbance (ED)*? What are the relative risks of students from each racial/ethnic group being classified with an *Emotional Disturbance* compared to all other students?

	American Indian or Alaskan Native	Asian or Pacific Islander	Black or African American	Hispanic or Latino	White	Multiracial	Total
Student Enrollment	A	B	C	D	E	F	G
Emotional Disturbance (ED)	H	I	J	K	L	M	N
Risk Index	H ÷ A × 100 =	I ÷ B × 100 =	J ÷ C × 100 =	K ÷ D × 100 =	L ÷ E × 100 =	M ÷ F × 100 =	N ÷ G × 100 =
Relative Risk	(H ÷ A) ÷ [(N − H) ÷ (G − A)] =	(I ÷ B) ÷ [(N − Q) ÷ (G − B)] =	(J ÷ C) ÷ [(N − J) ÷ (G − C)] =	(K ÷ D) ÷ [(N − K) ÷ (G − D)] =	(L ÷ E) ÷ [(N − L) ÷ (G − E)] =	(M ÷ F) ÷ [(N − M) ÷ (G − F)] =	

Students Classified With a Learning Disability (LD)

9. How many students are classified with a *Learning Disability (LD)*?

	American Indian or Alaskan Native	Asian or Pacific Islander	Black or African American	Hispanic or Latino	White	Multiracial	Total
Learning Disability (LD)	A	B	C	D	E	F	G

10. What is the composition of the students classified with a *Learning Disability (LD)*?

	American Indian or Alaskan Native	Asian or Pacific Islander	Black or African American	Hispanic or Latino	White	Multiracial	Total
Learning Disability (LD)	A ÷ G × 100 =	B ÷ G × 100 =	C ÷ G × 100 =	D ÷ G × 100 =	E ÷ G × 100 =	F ÷ G × 100 =	100%

11. What is the risk index (classification rate) of students from each racial/ethnic group being classified with a *Learning Disability (LD)*? What are the relative risks of students from each racial/ethnic group being classified with a *Learning Disability (LD)* compared to all other students?

	American Indian or Alaskan Native	Asian or Pacific Islander	Black or African American	Hispanic or Latino	White	Multiracial	Total
Student Enrollment	A	B	C	D	E	F	G
Learning Disability (LD)	H	I	J	K	L	M	N
Risk Index	H ÷ A × 100 =	I ÷ B × 100 =	J ÷ C × 100 =	K ÷ D × 100 =	L ÷ E × 100 =	M ÷ F × 100 =	N ÷ G × 100 =
Relative Risk	(H ÷ A) ÷ [(N – H) ÷ (G – A)] =	(I ÷ B) ÷ [(N – Q) ÷ (G – B)] =	(J ÷ C) ÷ [(N – J) ÷ (G – C)] =	(K ÷ D) ÷ [(N – K) ÷ (G – D)] =	(L ÷ E) ÷ [(N – L) ÷ (G – E)] =	(M ÷ F) ÷ [(N – M) ÷ (G – F)] =	

Students Classified With a Speech or Language Impairment (SI)

12. How many students are classified with a *Speech or Language Impairment (SI)*?

	American Indian or Alaskan Native	Asian or Pacific Islander	Black or African American	Hispanic or Latino	White	Multiracial	Total
Speech or Language Impairment (SI)	A	B	C	D	E	F	G

13. What is the composition of the students classified with a *Speech or Language Impairment (SI)*?

	American Indian or Alaskan Native	Asian or Pacific Islander	Black or African American	Hispanic or Latino	White	Multiracial	Total
Speech or Language Impairment (SI)	A ÷ G × 100 =	B ÷ G × 100 =	C ÷ G × 100 =	D ÷ G × 100 =	E ÷ G × 100 =	F ÷ G × 100 =	100%

14. What is the risk index (classification rate) of students from each racial/ethnic group being classified with a *Speech or Language Impairment (SI)*? What are the relative risks of students from each racial/ethnic group being classified with a *Speech or Language Impairment (SI)* compared to all other students?

	American Indian or Alaskan Native	Asian or Pacific Islander	Black or African American	Hispanic or Latino	White	Multiracial	Total
Student Enrollment	A	B	C	D	E	F	G
Speech or Language Impairment (SI)	H	I	J	K	L	M	N
Risk Index	H ÷ A × 100 =	I ÷ B × 100 =	J ÷ C × 100 =	K ÷ D × 100 =	L ÷ E × 100 =	M ÷ F × 100 =	N ÷ G × 100 =
Relative Risk	(H ÷ A) ÷ [(N − H) ÷ (G − A)] =	(I ÷ B) ÷ [(N − Q) ÷ (G − B)] =	(J ÷ C) ÷ [(N − J) ÷ (G − C)] =	(K ÷ D) ÷ [(N − K) ÷ (G − D)] =	(L ÷ E) ÷ [(N − L) ÷ (G − E)] =	(M ÷ F) ÷ [(N − M) ÷ (G − F)] =	

Reflection

Data Tool Patterns	Identify Group(s)	Designation
Enrollment percentage is higher than classification percentage		Underclassification
Enrollment percentage is lower than classification percentage		Overclassification
Enrollment percentage within range (1%–10%) of classification percentage		Proportional
Relative risk ratio higher than 1.5		Elevated risk ratio
Relative risk ratio lower than 0.75		Reduced risk ratio

Copyright © 2017 by Corwin. All rights reserved. Reprinted from *Solving Disproportionality and Achieving Equity: A Leader's Guide to Using Data to Change Hearts and Minds* by Edward Fergus. Thousand Oaks, CA: Corwin, www.corwin.com. Reproduction authorized only for the local school site or nonprofit organization that has purchased this book.

Level 2 Analysis: Process Data

The Early Intervention and Classification Process

Purpose: Articulate your district/school's early intervention and classification process by considering the path taken by a student who is exhibiting academic and behavior problems/needs in a classroom.

Directions: Please discuss this student's journey through the early intervention and special education classification process and record the following: *(1) key policies and practices that may affect or determine the student's outcome; (2) critical questions about bias that should be considered; and (3) possible gaps.*

	Stage 1: A student in the general education population is exhibiting an academic and/or behavioral need	Stage 2: A school-based committee considers the student referral and outline subsequent intervention series	Stage 3: The student is evaluated by a specialist depending on the need that is exhibited	Stage 4: The student receives an individual education plan (IEP) and outlines a least restrictive plan
What are your school's policies and practices at each stage?				
What are some questions about bias belief that should be asked at each stage?	E.g., are there common social identities (i.e., race, gender, FRLP) found among students referred?	E.g., does the intervention sequence isolate and/or punish student for extended time?	E.g., does the evaluation process consider cultural artifacts or processes as examples of assets?	E.g., does the IEP, when appropriate, focus on the least isolating context?
What are some possible gaps of each stage?				

The Available Interventions

Purpose: Articulate your district/school's available interventions for a student who is exhibiting an academic problem/need in a classroom.

Directions: Please discuss range of available interventions and implementation.

	Stage 1: List of available interventions by tiers—*create this list by content area.*	Stage 2: Define timing of interventions: How long have these interventions been implemented?	Stage 3: Define the location of interventions: Are these interventions commonly available and used by all practitioners?
Tier 1			
Tier 2			
Tier 3			

Copyright © 2017 by Corwin. All rights reserved. Reprinted from *Solving Disproportionality and Achieving Equity: A Leader's Guide to Using Data to Change Hearts and Minds* by Edward Fergus. Thousand Oaks, CA: Corwin, www.corwin.com. Reproduction authorized only for the local school site or nonprofit organization that has purchased this book.

Review Academic Referral Form

Purpose: Review your district/school's referral form in relation to outcome data.

Directions: Please discuss gaps in academic referral form and its translation/interpretation.

Given findings in the tables for items 21 and 22, identify the type of information the referral form requires. For example, does the form require explanation of Tier 1 interventions?	

Copyright © 2017 by Corwin. All rights reserved. Reprinted from *Solving Disproportionality and Achieving Equity: A Leader's Guide to Using Data to Change Hearts and Minds* by Edward Fergus. Thousand Oaks, CA: Corwin, www.corwin.com. Reproduction authorized only for the local school site or nonprofit organization that has purchased this book.

Level 3 Analysis: Outcome + Process Data = Root Causes

Identify Process Gaps	Identify How Process Gaps Lead to Outcomes	Preliminary Remedies of Process Gaps

Copyright © 2017 by Corwin. All rights reserved. Reprinted from *Solving Disproportionality and Achieving Equity: A Leader's Guide to Using Data to Change Hearts and Minds* by Edward Fergus. Thousand Oaks, CA: Corwin, www.corwin.com. Reproduction authorized only for the local school site or nonprofit organization that has purchased this book.

Root Cause Analysis 2: Disproportionality in Gifted, AP, Honors, and/or Accelerated Programs

The federal legislation regarding gifted and talented students acknowledges, "Students with talent are found in all cultural groups, across all economic strata, and in all areas of human endeavor" (Legislation, Regulations, and Guidance, 2006). Although this acknowledgement exists, there is wide variation in who is receiving gifted and talented programming. The disproportionality analysis in this section goes beyond gifted and talented, which is primarily an elementary school component, and includes middle and high school accelerated and AP/honors courses. This initial look at your school's or district's gifted, talented, AP, honors, and accelerated program enrollment data is meant to provide both a framework to examine equity in outcomes and to help your team pose questions about your school's or district's referral and enrollment policies and practices.

Level 1 Analysis: Outcome Data

Using your school's data, complete the following tables and answer the reflection questions.

Enrollment of Students in Gifted Programs (Elementary Grades K–5)

1. How many students are enrolled in district/school and gifted program by race/ethnicity (count of students)?

	American Indian or Alaskan Native	Asian or Pacific Islander	Black or African American	Hispanic or Latino	White	Multiracial	Total
Number of students in gifted program	A	B	C	D	E	F	G
Number of students enrolled in district (K–5 only)	H	I	J	K	L	M	N

2. What is the composition of students enrolled in gifted program by race/ethnicity (percent students)?

	American Indian or Alaskan Native	Asian or Pacific Islander	Black or African American	Hispanic or Latino	White (not of Hispanic Origin)	Multiracial	Total
Composition of students enrolled in gifted program	$A \div G \times 100 =$	$B \div G \times 100 =$	$C \div G \times 100 =$	$D \div G \times 100 =$	$E \div G \times 100 =$	$F \div G \times 100 =$	100%
Composition of students enrolled in district (K–5 only)	$H \div N \times 100 =$	$I \div N \times 100 =$	$J \div N \times 100 =$	$K \div N \times 100 =$	$L \div N \times 100 =$	$M \div N \times 100 =$	100%
Relative risk ratio of students enrolled in district/school to be gifted	$(A \div H) \div [(G - A) \div (N - H)] =$	$(B \div I) \div [(G - B) \div (N - Q)] =$	$(C \div J) \div [(G - C) \div (N - J)] =$	$(D \div K) \div [(G - D) \div (N - K)] =$	$(E \div L) \div [(G - E) \div (N - L)] =$	$(M \div F) \div [(G - F) \div (N - M)] =$	

3. How many students are enrolled in gifted program by gender (count students)?

	Male	Female	Total
Number of students in gifted program	A	B	C
Number of students enrolled in district (K–5 only)	H	I	J

4. What is the composition of students enrolled in gifted program by gender (percentage of students)?

	Male	Female	Total
Composition of students (percentage)	$A \div C \times 100 =$	$B \div C \times 100 =$	100%
Composition of students in district (K–5 only)	$H \div J \times 100 =$	$I \div J \times 100 =$	100%

5. How many students enrolled in gifted program by English Language Learner (ELL) status (count students)?

	ELL	Non-ELL	Total
Number of students	A	B	C
Number of students (K–5 only)	H	I	J

6. What is the composition of students enrolled in gifted program by English Language Learner (ELL) status (percentage of students)?

	ELL	Non-ELL	Total
Composition of students (percentage)	$A \div C \times 100 =$	$B \div C \times 100 =$	100%
Composition of students (K–5 only)	$H \div J \times 100 =$	$I \div J \times 100 =$	100%

Enrollment of Students in Gifted, Honors, and/or Accelerated Programs (Middle School Grades 6–8)

7. How many students are enrolled in gifted, honors, and/or accelerated programs by race/ethnicity (count students)?

	American Indian or Alaskan Native	Asian or Pacific Islander	Black or African American	Hispanic or Latino	White	Multiracial	Total
Number of students in gifted program	A	B	C	D	E	F	G
Number of students enrolled in district (6–8 only)	H	I	J	K	L	M	N

8. What is the composition of students enrolled in gifted, honors, and/or accelerated programs by race/ethnicity (percent students)?

	American Indian or Alaskan Native	Asian or Pacific Islander	Black or African American	Hispanic or Latino	White	Multiracial	Total
Composition of students enrolled in gifted program	$A \div G \times 100 =$	$B \div G \times 100 =$	$C \div G \times 100 =$	$D \div G \times 100 =$	$E \div G \times 100 =$	$F \div G \times 100 =$	100%
Composition of students enrolled in district (6–8 only)	$H \div N \times 100 =$	$I \div N \times 100 =$	$J \div N \times 100 =$	$K \div N \times 100 =$	$L \div N \times 100 =$	$M \div N \times 100 =$	100%
Relative risk of students enrolled in district/school to be gifted, AP/honors	$(A \div H) \div [(G-A) \div (N-H)] =$	$(B \div I) \div [(G-B) \div (N-Q)] =$	$(C \div J) \div [(G-C) \div (N-J)] =$	$(D \div K) \div [(G-D) \div (N-K)] =$	$(E \div L) \div [(G-E) \div (N-L)] =$	$(F \div M) \div [(G-F) \div (N-M)] =$	

9. How many students are enrolled in gifted, honors, and/or accelerated programs by gender (count students)?

	Male	Female	Total
Number of students in gifted program	A	B	C
Number of students enrolled in district (6–8 only)	H	I	J

10. What is the composition of students enrolled in gifted, honors, and/or accelerated programs by gender (percentage of students)?

	Male	Female	Total
Composition of students (percentage)	$A \div C \times 100 =$	$B \div C \times 100 =$	100%
Composition of students in district (6–8 only)	$H \div J \times 100 =$	$I \div J \times 100 =$	100%

11. How many students enrolled in gifted, honors, and/or accelerated programs by English Language Learner (ELL) status (count students)?

	ELL	Non-ELL	Total
Number of students	A	B	C
Number of students (6–8 only)	H	I	J

12. What is the composition of students enrolled in gifted, honors, and/or accelerated programs by English Language Learner (ELL) status (percentage of students)?

	ELL	Non-ELL	Total
Composition of students (percentage)	A ÷ C × 100 =	B ÷ C × 100 =	100%
Composition of students (6–8 only)	H ÷ J × 100 =	I ÷ J × 100 =	100%

Enrollment of Students in Gifted, AP, Honors, and/or Accelerated Programs (High School Grades 9–12)

13. How many students are enrolled in gifted, AP, honors, and/or accelerated programs by race/ethnicity (count students)?

	American Indian or Alaskan Native	Asian or Pacific Islander	Black or African American	Hispanic or Latino	White	Multiracial	Total
Number of students in AP or honors program	A	B	C	D	E	F	G
Number of students enrolled in district (9–12 only)	H	I	J	K	L	M	N

14. What is the composition of students enrolled in gifted, AP, honors, and/or accelerated programs by race/ethnicity (percentage students)?

	American Indian or Alaskan Native	Asian or Pacific Islander	Black or African American	Hispanic or Latino	White	Multiracial	Total
Composition of students enrolled in AP/honors program	A ÷ G × 100 =	B ÷ G × 100 =	C ÷ G × 100 =	D ÷ G × 100 =	E ÷ G × 100 =	F ÷ G × 100 =	100%
Composition of students enrolled in district/school (9–12 only)	H ÷ N × 100 =	I ÷ N × 100 =	J ÷ N × 100 =	K ÷ N × 100 =	L ÷ N × 100 =	M ÷ N × 100 =	100%
Relative risk ratio of students enrolled in district/school to be gifted, AP, honors, etc.	(A ÷ H) ÷ [(G − A) ÷ (N − H)] =	(B ÷ I) ÷ [(G − B) ÷ (N − Q)] =	(C ÷ J) ÷ [(G − C) ÷ (N − J)] =	(D ÷ K) ÷ [(G − D) ÷ (N − K)] =	(E ÷ L) ÷ [(G − E) ÷ (N − L)] =	(F ÷ M) ÷ [(G − F) ÷ (N − M)] =	

15. How many students are enrolled in gifted, AP, honors, and/or accelerated programs by gender (count students)?

	Male	Female	Total
Number of students in AP/honors program	A	B	C
Number of students enrolled in district (9–12 only)	H	I	J

16. What is the composition of students enrolled in gifted, AP, honors, and/or accelerated programs by gender (percentage of students)?

	Male	Female	Total
Composition of students in AP/honors (percentage)	A ÷ C × 100 =	B ÷ C × 100 =	100%
Composition of students in district (9–12 only)	H ÷ J × 100 =	I ÷ J × 100 =	100%

17. How many students enrolled in gifted, AP, honors, and/or accelerated programs by English Language Learner (ELL) status (count students)?

	ELL	Non-ELL	Total
Number of students in AP/honors	A	B	C
Number of students (9–12 only)	H	I	J

18. What is the composition of students enrolled in gifted, AP, honors, and/or accelerated programs by English Language Learner (ELL) status (percentage of students)?

	ELL	Non-ELL	Total
Composition of students in AP/honors (percentage)	A ÷ C × 100 =	B ÷ C × 100 =	100%
Composition of students (9–12 only)	H ÷ J × 100 =	I ÷ J × 100 =	100%

19. What is the referral rate for academic interventions and referral to gifted, AP, honors, or accelerated programs from each racial/ethnic group?

	American Indian or Alaskan Native	Asian or Pacific Islander	Black or African American	Hispanic or Latino	White	Multiracial	Total
Number of students in school or district	A	B	C	D	E	F	G
Number of students referred for academic intervention	H	I	J	K	L	M	N
Number of students referred for gifted, AP, honors, etc.	O	P	Q	R	S	T	U
Risk index of students being referred for intervention	H ÷ A × 100 =	I ÷ B × 100 =	J ÷ C × 100 =	K ÷ D × 100 =	L ÷ E × 100 =	M ÷ F × 100 =	N ÷ G × 100 =
Risk index of students being referred for gifted, AP, honors, etc.	O ÷ A × 100 =	P ÷ B × 100 =	Q ÷ C × 100 =	R ÷ D × 100 =	Z ÷ E × 100 =	T ÷ F × 100 =	U ÷ G × 100 =

Comparing Compositions

20. What is the overall composition of the students being in gifted, AP, honors, etc. in your school or school district?

	American Indian or Alaskan Native	Asian or Pacific Islander	Black or African American	Hispanic or Latino	White	Multiracial	Total
Student enrollment[1] (Items 2, 8, and 14)							100%
Students in gifted, AP, honors, etc. programs (Items 2, 8, and 14)							100%
Risk index of being referred for intervention (Item 19)							100%
Risk index of being referred for gifted, AP, honors, etc. (Item 19)							

[1]This analysis should be modified based on whether it's a school or district level analysis. If it's school level, then you should take enrollment figures from the corresponding tables for items 1, 7, or 13. If it's district level, then you should take enrollment figures from all corresponding tables for items 1, 7, and 13.

Copyright © 2017 by Corwin. All rights reserved. Reprinted from *Solving Disproportionality and Achieving Equity: A Leader's Guide to Using Data to Change Hearts and Minds* by Edward Fergus. Thousand Oaks, CA: Corwin, www.corwin.com. Reproduction authorized only for the local school site or nonprofit organization that has purchased this book.

Achievement of Students in Gifted and Nongifted Programs (Grades 3–5)

21. What is the achievement students enrolled in gifted and nongifted programs by race/ethnicity (mean scale score on state assessment or appropriate assessment)?

	American Indian or Alaskan Native	Asian or Pacific Islander	Black or African American	Hispanic or Latino	White	Multiracial	Total
Mean scale score for students in gifted programs							
Mean scale score for students in nongifted programs							

Achievement of Students in Gifted and Nongifted Programs (Grades 6–8)

22. What is the achievement students enrolled in gifted and nongifted programs by race/ethnicity (mean scale score)?

	American Indian or Alaskan Native	Asian or Pacific Islander	Black or African American	Hispanic or Latino	White	Multiracial	Total
Mean scale score or GPA for students in gifted programs							
Mean scale score or GPA for students in nongifted programs							

Achievement of Students in Gifted and
Nongifted Programs (Grades 9–12)

23. What is the achievement students enrolled in gifted and nongifted pro-
    grams by race/ethnicity (mean scale score)?

	American Indian or Alaskan Native	Asian or Pacific Islander	Black or African American	Hispanic or Latino	White	Multiracial	Total
Mean GPA for students in gifted programs							
Mean GPA for students in nongifted programs							

Copyright © 2017 by Corwin. All rights reserved. Reprinted from *Solving Disproportionality and Achieving Equity: A Leader's Guide to Using Data to Change Hearts and Minds* by Edward Fergus. Thousand Oaks, CA: Corwin, www.corwin.com. Reproduction authorized only for the local school site or nonprofit organization that has purchased this book.

Reflection

Data Tool Patterns	Identify Group(s)	Designation
Enrollment percentage is higher than gifted program percentage		Underrepresentation
Enrollment percentage is lower than gifted program percentage		Overrepresentation
Enrollment percentage within range (1%–10%) of gifted program percentage		Proportional
Relative risk ratio higher than 1.5		Elevated risk ratio
Relative risk ratio lower than 0.75		Reduced risk ratio

Copyright © 2017 by Corwin. All rights reserved. Reprinted from *Solving Disproportionality and Achieving Equity: A Leader's Guide to Using Data to Change Hearts and Minds* by Edward Fergus. Thousand Oaks, CA: Corwin, www.corwin.com. Reproduction authorized only for the local school site or nonprofit organization that has purchased this book.

Level 2 Analysis: Process Data

The Elementary Level Gifted Identification Process

Purpose: Articulate your district/school's identification process by considering the path taken by a student.

Directions: Please discuss this student's journey through the identification process and record the following: *(1) key policies and practices that may affect or determine the student's outcome, (2) critical questions about bias that should be considered, and (3) possible gaps.*

	Process Element 1: Criteria used to identify students eligible for program	Process Element 2: Communication about the program and its criteria	Process Element 3: The opportunities for interaction between students in gifted programs and those in nongifted programs
What are your district/school's policies and practices regarding this process element?			
What are some questions about bias belief that should be asked about this process element?	E.g., do the criteria favor one form of learning and learning expression over others?	E.g., are communication strategies differed by community members?	E.g., are students given opportunities to integrate throughout the school day?
What are some possible gaps of each process element?			

Copyright © 2017 by Corwin. All rights reserved. Reprinted from *Solving Disproportionality and Achieving Equity: A Leader's Guide to Using Data to Change Hearts and Minds* by Edward Fergus. Thousand Oaks, CA: Corwin, www.corwin.com. Reproduction authorized only for the local school site or nonprofit organization that has purchased this book.

Level 2 Analysis: Process Data

The Middle School Level Gifted, Honors, or Accelerated Identification Process

Purpose: Articulate your district/school's identification process by considering the path taken by a student.

Directions: Please discuss this student's journey through the identification process and record the following: *(1) key policies and practices that may affect or determine the student's outcome, (2) critical questions about bias that should be considered, and (3) possible gaps.*

	Process Element 1: Criteria used to identify students eligible for program	Process Element 2: Communication about the program and its criteria	Process Element 3: The opportunities for interaction between students in gifted programs and those in nongifted programs
What are your district/school's policies and practices regarding this process element?			
What are some questions about bias belief that should be asked about this process element?	E.g., do the criteria favor one form of learning and learning expression over others?	E.g., are communication strategies differed by community members?	E.g., are students given opportunities to integrate throughout the school day?
What are some possible gaps of each process element?			

Copyright © 2017 by Corwin. All rights reserved. Reprinted from *Solving Disproportionality and Achieving Equity: A Leader's Guide to Using Data to Change Hearts and Minds* by Edward Fergus. Thousand Oaks, CA: Corwin, www.corwin.com. Reproduction authorized only for the local school site or nonprofit organization that has purchased this book.

Level 2 Analysis: Process Data

The High School Level AP, Honors, or Accelerated Identification Process

Purpose: Articulate your district/school's identification process by considering the path taken by a student.

Directions: Please discuss this student's journey through the identification process and record the following: *(1) key policies and practices that may affect or determine the student's outcome, (2) critical questions about bias that should be considered, and (3) possible gaps.*

	Process Element 1: Criteria used to identify students eligible for program	Process Element 2: Communication about the program and its criteria	Process Element 3: The opportunities for interaction between students in gifted programs and those in nongifted programs
What are your district/ school's policies and practices regarding this process element?			
What are some questions about bias belief that should be asked about this process element?	E.g., do the criteria favor one form of learning and learning expression over others?	E.g., are communication strategies differed by community members?	E.g., are students given opportunities to integrate throughout the school day?
What are some possible gaps of each process element?			

Copyright © 2017 by Corwin. All rights reserved. Reprinted from *Solving Disproportionality and Achieving Equity: A Leader's Guide to Using Data to Change Hearts and Minds* by Edward Fergus. Thousand Oaks, CA: Corwin, www.corwin.com. Reproduction authorized only for the local school site or nonprofit organization that has purchased this book.

Level 3 Analysis: Outcome + Process Data = Root Causes

Identify Process Gaps	Identify How Process Gaps Lead to Outcomes	Preliminary Remedies of Process Gaps

Copyright © 2017 by Corwin. All rights reserved. Reprinted from *Solving Disproportionality and Achieving Equity: A Leader's Guide to Using Data to Change Hearts and Minds* by Edward Fergus. Thousand Oaks, CA: Corwin, www.corwin.com. Reproduction authorized only for the local school site or nonprofit organization that has purchased this book.

Root Cause Analysis 3: Disproportionality in Discipline and Behavioral Supports

Aside from the 2004 IDEA reauthorization in which the state performance plan indicators 4a and 4b require examination of discipline rates for students with disabilities and the Office for Civil Rights CRDC data collection, there is no other federal mandate regarding the documentation of discipline data. Each state collects different types of discipline data, using different metrics. For example, some states (New York, New Jersey) collect at the state-level only "most violent" events (violence, vandalism, bullying); other states (e.g., California and Texas) collect information on the infraction and related consequences; and some mandate reporting of certain infractions such as corporal punishment at the state level (e.g., Louisiana). Despite this variation, most schools and districts collect a high level of detailed information about discipline and behavioral supports; however, the related analysis of this information generally stays at the level of "how many kids were suspended this month."

Discipline data are often times difficult to interpret because they can be tabulated in two different ways: by student and by referral. Student data count each student for whom there is a discipline record regardless of how many times the student has been referred. Referral data count the total number of infractions, but do not take into account that certain students are counted multiple times. As such, these two perspectives provide different information. Given this difference, the following is a basic framework for analyzing your school's discipline data. It looks at the following four areas: (1) the demographics of those students involved in your school's discipline process, (2) the types of discipline infractions, (3) the outcomes of those infractions, and (4) the recidivism of suspensions.

Level 1 Analysis: Outcome Data

Using your school's data, complete the following tables and answer the reflection questions.

Enrollment of Students Receiving a Disciplinary Referral

1. How many students are referred for disciplinary action by race/ethnicity (count students)?

	American Indian or Alaskan Native	Asian or Pacific Islander	Black or African American	Hispanic or Latino	White	Multiracial	Total
Number of students referred for disciplinary action	A	B	C	D	E	F	G
Number of students enrolled in district/ school	H	I	J	K	L	M	N

2. What is the composition of students referred for disciplinary action by race/ethnicity (count students)?

	American Indian or Alaskan Native	Asian or Pacific Islander	Black or African American	Hispanic or Latino	White	Multiracial	Total
Composition of students referred for disciplinary action	$A \div G \times 100 =$	$B \div G \times 100 =$	$C \div G \times 100 =$	$D \div G \times 100 =$	$E \div G \times 100 =$	$F \div G \times 100 =$	100%
Composition of students enrolled in district/school	$H \div N \times 100 =$	$I \div N \times 100 =$	$J \div N \times 100 =$	$K \div N \times 100 =$	$L \div N \times 100 =$	$M \div N \times 100 =$	100%
Composition of students within group reflected by referrals for disciplinary action	$A \div H \times 100 =$	$B \div I \times 100 =$	$C \div J \times 100 =$	$D \div K \times 100 =$	$E \div L \times 100 =$	$F \div M \times 100 =$	
Relative risk ratio of students receiving a disciplinary referral	$(A \div H) \div [(G - A) \div (N - H)] =$	$(B \div I) \div [(G - B) \div (N - Q)] =$	$(C \div J) \div [(G - C) \div (N - J)] =$	$(D \div K) \div [(G - D) \div (N - K)] =$	$(E \div L) \div [(G - E) \div (N - L)] =$	$(F \div M) \div [(G - F) \div (N - M)] =$	

3. How many students referred for disciplinary action by gender (count students)?

	Male	Female	Total
Number of students	A	B	C

4. What is the composition of students referred for disciplinary action by gender (percentage of students)?

	Male	Female	Total
Composition of students (percentage)	A ÷ C × 100 =	B ÷ C × 100 =	100%

5. How many students are referred for disciplinary action by grade level (count students)?

	Kindergarten to 5th	6th to 8th	9th to 12th	Total
Number of students	A	B	C	D

6. What is the composition of students referred for disciplinary action by grade level (percentage of students)?

	Kindergarten to 5th	6th to 8th	9th to 12th	Total
Composition of students (percentage)	A ÷ D × 100 =	B ÷ D × 100 =	C ÷ D × 100 =	100%

Count of Disciplinary Referrals

7. How many disciplinary referrals were written by race/ethnicity?

	American Indian or Alaskan Native	Asian or Pacific Islander	Black or African American	Hispanic or Latino	White	Multiracial	Total
Number of disciplinary referrals	A	B	C	D	E	F	G

8. What is the composition of disciplinary referrals (count referrals)?

	American Indian or Alaskan Native	Asian or Pacific Islander	Black or African American	Hispanic or Latino	White	Multiracial	Total
Composition of disciplinary referrals	A ÷ G × 100 =	B ÷ G × 100 =	C ÷ G × 100 =	D ÷ G × 100 =	E ÷ G × 100 =	F ÷ G × 100 =	100%

9. How many disciplinary referrals were written by gender?

	Male	Female	Total
Number of disciplinary referrals	A	B	C

10. What is the composition of disciplinary referrals by gender (count referrals)?

	Male	Female	Total
Composition of disciplinary referrals	$A \div C \times 100 =$	$B \div C \times 100 =$	100%

11. How many disciplinary referrals were written by grade level?

	Kindergarten to 5th	6th to 8th	9th to 12th	Total
Number of disciplinary referrals	A	B	C	D

12. What is the composition of disciplinary referrals by grade level (count referrals)?

	Kindergarten to 5th	6th to 8th	9th to 12th	Total
Composition of disciplinary referrals	$A \div D \times 100 =$	$B \div D \times 100 =$	$C \div D \times 100 =$	100%

Copyright © 2017 by Corwin. All rights reserved. Reprinted from *Solving Disproportionality and Achieving Equity: A Leader's Guide to Using Data to Change Hearts and Minds* by Edward Fergus. Thousand Oaks, CA: Corwin, www.corwin.com. Reproduction authorized only for the local school site or nonprofit organization that has purchased this book.

Reflection

Data Tool Patterns	Identify Group(s)	Designation
Enrollment percentage is higher than behavioral referral percentage		Underreferral
Enrollment percentage is lower than behavioral referral percentage		Overreferral
Enrollment percentage within range (1%–10%) of behavioral referral percentage		Proportional
Relative risk ratio higher than 1.5		Elevated risk ratio
Relative risk ratio lower than 0.75		Reduced risk ratio

Copyright © 2017 by Corwin. All rights reserved. Reprinted from *Solving Disproportionality and Achieving Equity: A Leader's Guide to Using Data to Change Hearts and Minds* by Edward Fergus. Thousand Oaks, CA: Corwin, www.corwin.com. Reproduction authorized only for the local school site or nonprofit organization that has purchased this book.

Reason for Referral

13. What were the five most cited reasons for disciplinary referrals?

	Referral Type	American Indian or Alaskan Native	Asian or Pacific Islander	Black or African American	Hispanic or Latino	White	Multiracial	Total Referrals
Most common								
2nd most common								
3rd most common								
4th most common								
5th most common								

14. What were the five most cited reasons for disciplinary referrals by gender?

	Referral Type	Male	Female	Total Referrals
Most common				
2nd most common				
3rd most common				
4th most common				
5th most common				

15. What were the five most cited reasons for disciplinary referrals by grade level?

	Referral Type	Kindergarten to 5th	6th to 8th	9th to 12th	Total Referrals
Most common					
2nd most common					
3rd most common					
4th most common					
5th most common					

Copyright © 2017 by Corwin. All rights reserved. Reprinted from *Solving Disproportionality and Achieving Equity: A Leader's Guide to Using Data to Change Hearts and Minds* by Edward Fergus. Thousand Oaks, CA: Corwin, www.corwin.com. Reproduction authorized only for the local school site or nonprofit organization that has purchased this book.

Reflection and Interpretation

Outcome Data Interpretation Questions	
Are different groups of students referred for different reasons? If so, why do you think that is?	
What is the relationship between the most common reasons for referrals and the referrals most likely to result in suspensions? What does this tell you about your school's discipline policies and practices?	
Insert other interpretation questions:	
Insert other interpretation questions:	

Copyright © 2017 by Corwin. All rights reserved. Reprinted from *Solving Disproportionality and Achieving Equity: A Leader's Guide to Using Data to Change Hearts and Minds* by Edward Fergus. Thousand Oaks, CA: Corwin, www.corwin.com. Reproduction authorized only for the local school site or nonprofit organization that has purchased this book.

Multiple Referrals

16. What is the percentage of students who received one or more multiple referrals?

	American Indian or Alaskan Native	Asian or Pacific Islander	Black or African American	Hispanic or Latino	White	Multiracial	Total
Percentage of students who received more than *one* referral							
Percentage of students who received more than *three* referrals							
Percentage of students who received more than *five* referrals							

17. What is the percentage of students by gender who received one or more multiple referrals?

	Male	Female	Total
Percentage of students who received more than *one* referral			
Percentage of students who received more than *three* referrals			
Percentage of students who received more than *five* referrals			

18. What is the percentage of students by grade level who received one or more multiple referrals?

	Kindergarten to 5th	6th to 8th	9th to 12th	Total
Percentage of students who received more than *one* referral				
Percentage of students who received more than *three* referrals				
Percentage of students who received more than *five* referrals				

Copyright © 2017 by Corwin. All rights reserved. Reprinted from *Solving Disproportionality and Achieving Equity: A Leader's Guide to Using Data to Change Hearts and Minds* by Edward Fergus. Thousand Oaks, CA: Corwin, www.corwin.com. Reproduction authorized only for the local school site or nonprofit organization that has purchased this book.

Reflection and Interpretation

Outcome Data Interpretation Questions	
Are different groups of students experiencing different recidivism rates? If so, why do you think that is?	
What does the recidivism rate tell you about your district/school's discipline policies and practices?	
Insert other interpretation questions:	
Insert other interpretation questions:	

Copyright © 2017 by Corwin. All rights reserved. Reprinted from *Solving Disproportionality and Achieving Equity: A Leader's Guide to Using Data to Change Hearts and Minds* by Edward Fergus. Thousand Oaks, CA: Corwin, www.corwin.com. Reproduction authorized only for the local school site or nonprofit organization that has purchased this book.

Action or Consequences

19. What were the five most cited actions or consequences for disciplinary referrals?

	Action Type	American Indian or Alaskan Native	Asian or Pacific Islander	Black or African American	Hispanic or Latino	White	Multiracial	Total Actions
Most common								
2nd most common								
3rd most common								
4th most common								
5th most common								

20. What were the five most cited actions or consequences for disciplinary referrals by gender and grade?

	Action Type	Male	Female	Total Actions
Most common				
2nd most common				
3rd most common				
4th most common				
5th most common				

21. What were the five most cited actions or consequences for disciplinary referrals by gender and grade?

	Action Type	Kindergarten to 5th	6th to 8th	9th to 12th	Total Actions
Most common					
2nd most common					
3rd most common					
4th most common					
5th most common					

Copyright © 2017 by Corwin. All rights reserved. Reprinted from *Solving Disproportionality and Achieving Equity: A Leader's Guide to Using Data to Change Hearts and Minds* by Edward Fergus. Thousand Oaks, CA: Corwin, www.corwin.com. Reproduction authorized only for the local school site or nonprofit organization that has purchased this book.

Level 2 Analysis: Process Data

The School Discipline Process

Purpose: Articulate your district/school's discipline process by considering the path taken by a student who is exhibiting behavior problems/needs in a classroom.

Directions: Please discuss this student's journey through the discipline process and record the following: *(1) key policies and practices that may affect or determine the student's outcome, (2) critical questions about bias that should be considered, and (3) possible gaps.*

	Stage 1: Student exhibits problem behavior/need and teacher submits a referral to the site administrator for he or him to consider.	Stage 2: The site administrator receives and evaluates the behavioral referral.	Stage 3: The site administrator recommends student be suspended and/or subsequent intervention series.
What are your school's policies and practices at each stage?			
What are some questions about bias belief that should be asked at each stage?	E.g., are there common social identities (i.e., race, gender, FRLP) found among students referred?	E.g., does the evaluation process consider cultural artifacts or processes as antecedents to the infraction situation?	E.g., does the intervention sequence isolate and/or punish student for extended time?
What are some possible gaps of each stage?			

Copyright © 2017 by Corwin. All rights reserved. Reprinted from *Solving Disproportionality and Achieving Equity: A Leader's Guide to Using Data to Change Hearts and Minds* by Edward Fergus. Thousand Oaks, CA: Corwin, www.corwin.com. Reproduction authorized only for the local school site or nonprofit organization that has purchased this book.

Level 2 Analysis: Process Data

The Available Interventions

Purpose: Articulate your district/school's available interventions for a student who is exhibiting an academic problem/need in a classroom.[2]

Directions: Please discuss range of available interventions and implementation.

	Stage 1: List of available interventions by tiers—*create this list by content area.*	Stage 2: Define timing of interventions—how long have these interventions been implemented?	Stage 3: Define the location of interventions—are these interventions commonly available and used by all practitioners?
Tier 1: School/classroom wide systems for all students, staff, and settings			
Tier 2: Specialized group for students who are demonstrating at-risk behavior (i.e., periodic behavior but not consistent)			
Tier 3: Specialized group for students who are demonstrating high-risk behavior (i.e., consistent behavior when specific triggers are present)			

[2]Adapted from www.pbis.org. Considerations for behavioral interventions: (1) teaching and reinforcing context-appropriate social behaviors or skills; (2) removing antecedent factors that trigger occurrences of problem behavior; (3) adding antecedent factors that trigger occurrences of context-appropriate social skills; (4) removing consequence factors that maintain (function) occurrences of problem behaviors; (5) adding consequence factors that maintain occurrences of context-appropriate social behaviors.

Copyright © 2017 by Corwin. All rights reserved. Reprinted from *Solving Disproportionality and Achieving Equity: A Leader's Guide to Using Data to Change Hearts and Minds* by Edward Fergus. Thousand Oaks, CA: Corwin, www.corwin.com. Reproduction authorized only for the local school site or nonprofit organization that has purchased this book.

Level 2 Analysis: Process Data

Effectiveness of Interventions

Purpose: Articulate your district/school's intervention effectiveness for a student who is exhibiting an academic problem/need in a classroom.

Directions: Please discuss intervention effectiveness and demonstrate evidence.

Intervention Level	What are the most effective interventions and why? Demonstrate evidence of effectiveness.
Tier 1 **School/classroomwide systems for all students, staff, and settings**	
Tier 2 **Specialized group for students demonstrating at-risk behavior**	
Tier 3 **Specialized group for students demonstrating high-risk behavior**	

Copyright © 2017 by Corwin. All rights reserved. Reprinted from *Solving Disproportionality and Achieving Equity: A Leader's Guide to Using Data to Change Hearts and Minds* by Edward Fergus. Thousand Oaks, CA: Corwin, www.corwin.com. Reproduction authorized only for the local school site or nonprofit organization that has purchased this book.

Level 2 Analysis: Process Data

Review Code of Conduct

Purpose: Review your district/school's code of conduct in relation to outcome data.

Directions: Please discuss gaps in code of conduct translation/interpretation.

Given findings in the tables for items 13–15, examine how well the code of conduct provides explanation of each infraction/reason and its differentiations by grade level/age.	
Given findings in the tables for items 19–21, examine how well the code of conduct provides an outline of each infraction/reason and progressive ladder of actions or consequences.	

Copyright © 2017 by Corwin. All rights reserved. Reprinted from *Solving Disproportionality and Achieving Equity: A Leader's Guide to Using Data to Change Hearts and Minds* by Edward Fergus. Thousand Oaks, CA: Corwin, www.corwin.com. Reproduction authorized only for the local school site or nonprofit organization that has purchased this book.

Level 2 Analysis: Process Data

Review Behavioral Referral Form

Purpose: Review your district/school's referral form in relation to outcome data.

Directions: Please discuss gaps in behavioral referral form and its translation/interpretation.

Given findings in the tables for items 13–15, examine how well the referral form provides an opportunity for explanation of antecedents regarding infraction/reason.	
Given findings in the tables for items 19–21, examine how well the referral form provides an opportunity for documentation of actions or consequences previously attempted.	

Copyright © 2017 by Corwin. All rights reserved. Reprinted from *Solving Disproportionality and Achieving Equity: A Leader's Guide to Using Data to Change Hearts and Minds* by Edward Fergus. Thousand Oaks, CA: Corwin, www.corwin.com. Reproduction authorized only for the local school site or nonprofit organization that has purchased this book.

Level 3 Analysis: Outcome + Process Data = Root Causes

Identify Process Gaps	Identify How Process Gaps Lead to Outcomes	Preliminary Remedies of Process Gaps

Copyright © 2017 by Corwin. All rights reserved. Reprinted from *Solving Disproportionality and Achieving Equity: A Leader's Guide to Using Data to Change Hearts and Minds* by Edward Fergus. Thousand Oaks, CA: Corwin, www.corwin.com. Reproduction authorized only for the local school site or nonprofit organization that has purchased this book.

Summary of Common Root Causes

Now that you have some possible root causes, the form below is intended to help leadership map the root causes across the various disproportionality areas and a format for putting together a summary document to share with staff.

Root Causes	Evidence	Recommendations

Copyright © 2017 by Corwin. All rights reserved. Reprinted from *Solving Disproportionality and Achieving Equity: A Leader's Guide to Using Data to Change Hearts and Minds* by Edward Fergus. Thousand Oaks, CA: Corwin, www.corwin.com. Reproduction authorized only for the local school site or nonprofit organization that has purchased this book.

STEP 3: MONITORING EQUITY WORK:
3- TO 5-YEAR SPAN OF WORK

The process for goal setting can take various forms, such as an ad hoc equity team representing the school staff, or it could be the disproportionality leadership team. What I find most paramount about the process is ensuring that there are individuals in the room with the capacity to develop strategic goals and plans. This capacity is critical to make sure that the goals are manageable, challenge growth, and can be measured over the time period of the plan.

The outline in the proceeding pages is intended to make the team establish SMART goals, identify the indicators that will let them know they are heading in the right direction, establish discrete tasks for each month, and identify when to monitor the wellness of the plan versus simply outcomes.

Part 1: Identify SMART[3] Goal(s) and Indicators

Year-End SMART Goal(s)

What improvements (1) to how student behavior is managed, and (2) to student referral outcomes do you hope to make by the end of the school year? Make sure these goals align with the overall school culture and climate vision.

Examples:

By May 2017, 90% of office referrals will contain detail on misbehavior and behavior modification strategies attempted.

By May 2017, 90% of classroom observations will demonstrate positive/productive instruction talk between students and teachers.

By May 2017, 90% of school and classroom expectations (i.e., charts, reward activities) will include positive reinforcement language and strategies.

By May 2017, 100% of school staff will engage in developing school equity principles that include numerical, social justice, and cultural belief principles.

1. _____

2. _____

3. _____

4. _____

5. _____

---

[3] SMART—Specific, Measurable, Agreed Upon, Realistic, and Time-Based

Goal Indicators

How will you know whether or not you met your goal(s)? What specific changes will need to occur (regarding policies, systems, procedures, staff support, etc.)? How will you use culturally responsive principles to ensure equitable access and opportunity?

SMART Goal	Indicators	Equity Principles
Example: By May 2017, 90% of office referrals will contain detail on misbehavior and behavior modification strategies attempted.	1. PBIS team will (re)develop office referral form. 2. Office referrals will contain detail on misbehavior and behavior modification strategies.	• Seek proportional outcomes • Address deficit thinking • Address stereotypes and colorblindness
Example: By May 2017, 90% of classroom observations will demonstrate positive/ productive instruction talk between students and teachers.	1. Staff participate in monthly dialogue on positive/productive talk activities for the classroom. 2. Principal participates in monthly/ quarterly classroom visits focused on productive talk.	• Seek proportional outcomes • Address deficit thinking • Address stereotypes and colorblindness
Example: By May 2017, 90% of school and classroom expectations (i.e., charts, reward activities) will include positive reinforcement language and strategies.	1. Staff participate in training on positive reinforcement. 2. Staff participate in developing schoolwide and classroomwide expectations with positive reinforcement language.	• Seek proportional outcomes • Address deficit thinking • Address stereotypes and colorblindness
Example: By May 2017, 90% of PLC meetings will discuss instructional practice fidelity in terms of accuracy and consistency of practice.	1. Staff participate in training on defining fidelity in terms of accuracy and consistency. 2. PLC Teams progressively practice discussing and annotating fidelity accuracy and consistency on PLC forms. 3. Principal and Assistant Principal collect and review PLC meeting forms and notes.	• Seek proportional outcomes • Address deficit thinking • Address stereotypes and colorblindness

SMART Goal	Indicators	Equity Principles
		• Seek proportional outcomes • Address deficit thinking • Address stereotypes and colorblindness
		• Seek proportional outcomes • Address deficit thinking • Address stereotypes and colorblindness
		• Seek proportional outcomes • Address deficit thinking • Address stereotypes and colorblindness
		• Seek proportional outcomes • Address deficit thinking • Address stereotypes and colorblindness
		• Seek proportional outcomes • Address deficit thinking • Address stereotypes and colorblindness

Copyright © 2017 by Corwin. All rights reserved. Reprinted from *Solving Disproportionality and Achieving Equity: A Leader's Guide to Using Data to Change Hearts and Minds* by Edward Fergus. Thousand Oaks, CA: Corwin, www.corwin.com. Reproduction authorized only for the local school site or nonprofit organization that has purchased this book.

Part 2: Create a Task List

Tasks: Considering your indicators, what are some of the specific tasks that will need to be completed over the course of the year to reach your goal(s)? Your list is a working draft that will likely be revised as the year progresses. Your tasks don't have to be similar in size and scope.	People: Who will be responsible for completing the task?	Time: Approximately how much time will be needed to complete the task?	Data Collection: What data will be collected by this task?

Copyright © 2017 by Corwin. All rights reserved. Reprinted from *Solving Disproportionality and Achieving Equity: A Leader's Guide to Using Data to Change Hearts and Minds* by Edward Fergus. Thousand Oaks, CA: Corwin, www.corwin.com. Reproduction authorized only for the local school site or nonprofit organization that has purchased this book.

Part 3: Create a Timeline

Month	Completed Tasks: What tasks need be completed by the end of the (corresponding) month in to reach the year-end goal(s)?	Indicator Focus: Which year-end goal indicators do the tasks reflect?
August		
September		
October* Progress-monitoring activity should focus on wellness of task implementation		
November Progress monitor student interim outcomes		

Month	Completed Tasks: What tasks need be completed by the end of the (corresponding) month in to reach the year-end goal(s)?	Indicator Focus: Which year-end goal indicators do the tasks reflect?
December		
January* Progress-monitoring activity should focus on wellness of task implementation and student interim outcomes		
February		
March* Progress-monitoring activity should focus on wellness of task implementation and student interim outcomes		

Month	Completed Tasks: What tasks need be completed by the end of the (corresponding) month in to reach the year-end goal(s)?	Indicator Focus: Which year-end goal indicators do the tasks reflect?
April		
May* Progress-monitoring activity should focus on wellness of task implementation and student final outcomes		

*This is the approximate time for progressing monitoring by external partner and/or district team.

Copyright © 2017 by Corwin. All rights reserved. Reprinted from *Solving Disproportionality and Achieving Equity: A Leader's Guide to Using Data to Change Hearts and Minds* by Edward Fergus. Thousand Oaks, CA: Corwin, www.corwin.com. Reproduction authorized only for the local school site or nonprofit organization that has purchased this book.

STEP 4: PROGRESS-MONITORING TOOLS: MONTHLY DATA CALENDAR

The purpose of this early warning calendar is to provide a starting point for examining equity questions during monthly, quarterly, and annual data monitoring of outcomes and process. Additionally, this calendar provides guidance as to *what* questions to ask about data, as well as *what to do* with the answers. The intent of this calendar is to ensure equity questions are nonnegotiables in this process. Additionally, the perspective within this calendar includes an understanding that there are various points in the educational process in which racial/ethnic minority, low-income, and linguistically diverse populations are not receiving an equitable opportunity; thus the analysis questions that are posed are not only to monitor academic and behavioral outcomes early enough, but also represent an early warning or monitoring as to whether the educational process is a move toward being equitable and accessible.

Important Considerations

To use this document effectively as part of your leadership team meetings, intervention team meetings, etc., there has to be a robust data system. In addition, there needs to be a high-level data reliability. Another consideration to keep in mind is within the month-to-month analysis, there may be an issue of N size; in other words, sometimes the number of students may be too small to mean anything. In such cases, conducting a comparison analysis is highly relevant; in other words, asking comparison questions such as, "What percentage of the population does that constitute, does this look different or similar to other groups, etc.?"

Infrastructure and Process

1. Begin with district or building level leadership to conduct data analysis of this level. The purpose of these questions is to assist in guiding instructional management decisions.

2. Work with your data personnel to ascertain the following: the availability of database, the work involved in generating reports on these variables, the quality of the data entry, the consistency of data entry, etc. This is where the data and data system assessment in Chapter 3 is conducted.

3. The intent of the process is to assist your team to consistently understand the nature of student progress and its relationship to the wellness of process implementation.

Month	Practice/Process Events	Critical Process/Practice Questions	Available Data	Types of Analysis
SEPTEMBER	School attendance report	What is the daily attendance for all groups? Are there specific groups of students missing 1–3 days, and more than 4 days? How is tardiness marked by staff?	Attendance	Attendance patterns include tardiness and absences by gender, ELL status, special education status, race, and free or reduced lunch program (FRLP)
	Universal screenings	What are the skill levels across all groups and within groups (gender, race, and FRLP)? What percentage of students fall into each level of risk by groups (gender, race, and FRLP)? What are the research-based interventions? What is the wellness of intervention capacity?	DIBELS (example)	Number of students within each level of risk overall and by gender, ELL status, special education status, race, and FRLP
	Disciplinary referrals	What are the rates of disciplinary referrals? What are the average types of "offenses"? What are the interventions for these "offenses"? What are the location and time of day of "offenses"? Who is doing the referring?	Disciplinary referrals (or SWIS or other data systems)	Number of students referred for discipline overall and by gender, ELL status, special education status, race, and FRLP Percentage of students referred for discipline by groups (gender, ELL status, special education status, race, and FRLP)
	Course enrollment	What are the rates of course enrollments in the following classes: talented and gifted, advanced placement, honors, special education, and intervention services? What are the rates of course enrollments by race/ethnicity and gender?	Enrollment in talented and gifted, advanced placement, honors, special education, intervention services	Number of students enrolled in courses, placement, or service Percentage of students enrolled in course, placement, or services by groups (gender, ELL status, special education status, race, and FRLP)

Month	Practice/Process Events	Critical Process/Practice Questions	Available Data	Types of Analysis
OCTOBER	School attendance report	What is the daily attendance for all groups? Are there specific groups of students missing 1–3 days, and more than 4 days? How is tardiness marked by staff?	Attendance	Attendance patterns include tardiness and absences overall and by gender, ELL status, special education status, race, and FRLP
	5-week period report	What is the average grade across all groups (gender, race, and FRLP)? What is the average grade by classroom and content area? How are grades calculated during the 5-week period? Identify specific percentages (e.g., X% quizzes, Y% participation)	5-week report	Number and percentage of students getting As and Bs, Cs and Ds, and Fs Average grades by classroom and content overall and by gender, ELL status, special education status, race, and FRLP
	Disciplinary referrals	What are the rates of disciplinary referrals? What are the average types of "offenses"? What are the interventions for these "offenses"? What are the location and time of day of "offenses"? Who is doing the referring?	Disciplinary referrals	Number of students referred for discipline overall and by gender, ELL status, special education status, race, and FRLP Percentage of students referred for discipline by groups (gender, ELL status, special education status, race, and FRLP)
	Diagnostic screenings/ formative assessments	What are the skill levels across all groups and within groups (gender, race and FRLP)? What percentage of students fall into each level of risk by groups (gender, race, and FRLP)? How have participating students moved? What is the wellness of intervention capacity and implementation?	DIBELS (example)	Number of students within each level of risk overall and by gender, ELL status, special education status, race, and FRLP Percentage of students within each level moved up or down

Month	Practice/Process Events	Critical Process/Practice Questions	Available Data	Types of Analysis
NOVEMBER	School attendance report	What is the daily attendance for all groups? Are there specific groups of students missing 1–3 days, and more than 4 days? How is tardiness marked by staff?	Attendance	Attendance patterns include tardiness and absences overall and by gender, ELL status, special education status, race, and FRLP
	5-week period report	What is the average grade across all groups (gender, race, and FRLP)? What is the average grade by classroom and content area? How are grades calculated during the 5-week period? Identify specific percentages (e.g., X% quizzes, Y% participation)	5-week report	Number and percentage of students getting As and Bs, Cs and Ds, and Fs Average grades by classroom and content overall and by gender, ELL status, special education status, race, and FRLP
	Disciplinary referrals	What are the rates of disciplinary referrals? What are the average types of "offenses"? What are the interventions for these "offenses"? What are the location and time of day of "offenses"? Who is doing the referring?	Disciplinary referrals	Number of students referred for discipline overall and by gender, ELL status, special education status, race, and FRLP Percentage of students referred for discipline by groups (gender, ELL status, special education status, race, and FRLP)

Month	Practice/Process Events	Critical Process/Practice Questions	Available Data	Types of Analysis
DECEMBER	School attendance report	What is the daily attendance for all groups? Are there specific groups of students missing 1–3 days, and more than 4 days? How is tardiness marked by staff?	Attendance	Attendance patterns include tardiness and absences overall and by gender, ELL status, special education status, race, and FRLP
	5-week period report	What is the average grade across all groups (gender, race, and FRLP)? What is the average grade by classroom and content area? How are grades calculated during 5-week period? Identify specific percentages (e.g., X% quizzes, Y% participation)	5-week report	Number and percentage of students getting As and Bs, Cs and Ds, and Fs Average grades by classroom and content overall and by gender, ELL status, special education status, race, and FRLP
	Course grades	What is the average grade across all groups (gender, race, and FRLP)? What is the average grade by classroom and content area? Identify necessary support for teachers, coaching, PD, and training.	Semester grades	Number and percentage of students getting As and Bs, Cs and Ds, and Fs Average grades by classroom and content overall and by gender, ELL status, special education status, race, and FRLP
	Disciplinary referrals	What are the rates of disciplinary referrals? What are the average types of "offenses"? What are the interventions for these "offenses"? What are the laddered steps between referral and suspension? What is the percentage change in referrals and suspension? Ratio?	Disciplinary referrals	Number of students referred for discipline Percentage of students referred for discipline by groups (gender, ELL status, special education status, race, and FRLP)
	Diagnostic screenings/ formative assessments	What are the skill levels across all groups and within groups (gender, race and FRLP)? What percentage of students fall into each level of risk by groups (gender, race, and FRLP)? How have participating students moved? What is the wellness of intervention capacity and implementation?	DIBELS (example)	Number of students within each level of risk overall and by gender, ELL status, special education status, race, and FRLP Percentage of students within each level moved up or down

Month	Practice/Process Events	Critical Process/Practice Questions	Available Data	Types of Analysis
JANUARY	School attendance report	What is the daily attendance for all groups? Are there specific groups of students missing 1–3 days, and more than 4 days? How is tardiness marked by staff? How does the school's late policy impact attendance? What is the policy and interventions for cutting classes?	Attendance	Attendance patterns includes tardiness and absences overall and by gender, ELL status, special education status, race, and FRLP
	Course enrollment	What are the rates of course enrollments in the following classes: talented and gifted, advanced placement, honors, special education, and intervention services? What are the rates of course enrollments by race/ethnicity and gender? How do we create more inclusive opportunities?	Enrollment in talented and gifted, advanced placement, honors, special education, and intervention services	Number of students enrolled in courses, placement, or service Percentage of students enrolled in course, placement, or services by groups (gender, ELL status, special education status, race, and FRLP)
	Disciplinary referrals	What are the rates of disciplinary referrals? What are the average types of "offenses"? What are the interventions for these "offenses"? What are the laddered steps between referral and suspension? What is the percentage change in referrals and suspension? What is the ratio of referral to suspension?	Disciplinary referrals	Number of students referred for discipline overall and by gender, ELL status, special education status, race and FRLP Percentage of students referred for discipline by groups (gender, ELL status, special education status, race, and FRLP)

Month	Practice/Process Events	Critical Process/Practice Questions	Available Data	Types of Analysis
FEBRUARY	School attendance report	What is the daily attendance for all groups? Are there specific groups of students missing 1–3 days, and more than 4 days? How is tardiness marked by staff?	Attendance	Attendance patterns include tardiness and absences overall and by gender, ELL status, special education status, race, and FRLP
	Universal screenings/ formative assessments	What are the skill levels across all groups and within groups (gender, race, and FRLP)? What percentage of students fall into each level of risk by groups (gender, race, and FRLP)? How many have shown progress since the previous screening in September? What is the wellness of intervention capacity and implementation?	DIBELS (example)	Number of students within each level of risk overall and by gender, ELL status, special education status, race, and FRLP
	Disciplinary referrals	What are the rates of disciplinary referrals? What are the average types of "offenses"? What are the interventions for these "offenses"? What are the laddered steps between referral and suspensions? What is the percentage change in referrals and suspension? What is the ratio of referral to suspension?	Disciplinary referrals	Number of students referred for discipline overall and gender, ELL status, special education status, race and FRLP, and type of referral? Percentage of students referred for discipline by groups (gender, ELL status, special education status, race, and FRLP) and type of referral
	5-week period report	What is the average grade across all groups (gender, race, and FRLP)? What is the average grade by classroom and content area? How are grades calculated during 5-week period? Identify specific percentages (e.g., X% quizzes, Y% participation) How has instruction improved as a result of PD, coaching, and training?	5-week period report	Number and percentage of students getting As and Bs, Cs and Ds, and Fs Average grades by classroom and content overall and by gender, ELL status, special education status, race, and FRLP

Month	Practice/Process Events	Critical Process/Practice Questions	Available Data	Types of Analysis
MARCH	School attendance report	What is the daily attendance for all groups? Are there specific groups of students missing 1–3 days, and more than 4 days? How is tardiness marked by staff?	Attendance	Attendance patterns include tardiness and absences overall and by gender, ELL status, special education status, race, and FRLP
	5-week period report	What is the average grade across all groups (gender, race, and FRLP)? What is the average grade by classroom and content area? How are grades calculated during 5-week period? Identify specific percentages (e.g., X% quizzes, Y% participation)	5-week report	Number and percentage of students getting As and Bs, Cs and Ds, and Fs Average grades by classroom and content overall and by gender, ELL status, special education status, race, and FRLP
	Course grades	What is the average grade across all groups (gender, race, and FRLP)? What is the average grade by classroom and content area?	Semester grades	Number and percentage of students getting As and Bs, Cs and Ds, and Fs Average grades by classroom and content overall and by gender, ELL status, special education status, race, and FRLP
	Disciplinary referrals	What are the rates of disciplinary referrals? What are the average types of "offenses"? What are the interventions for these "offenses"? What are the location and time of day of "offenses"? Who is doing the referring?	Disciplinary referrals	Number of students referred for discipline Percentage of students referred for discipline by groups (gender, ELL status, special education status, race, and FRLP)

Month	Practice/Process Events	Critical Process/Practice Questions	Available Data	Types of Analysis
APRIL	School attendance report	What is the daily attendance for all groups? Are there specific groups of students missing 1–3 days, and more than 4 days? How is tardiness marked by staff?	Attendance	Attendance patterns include tardiness and absences overall and by gender, ELL status, special education status, race, and FRLP
	5-week period report	What is the average grade across all groups (gender, race, and FRLP)? What is the average grade by classroom and content area? How are grades calculated during 5-week period? Identify specific percentages (e.g., X% quizzes, Y% participation)	5-week report	Number and percentage of students getting As and Bs, Cs and Ds, and Fs Average grades by classroom and content overall and by gender, ELL status, special education status, race, and FRLP
	Disciplinary referrals	What are the rates of disciplinary referrals? What are the average types of "offenses"? What are the interventions for these "offenses"? What are the location and time of day of "offenses"? Who is doing the referring?	Disciplinary referrals	Number of students referred for discipline Percentage of students referred for discipline by groups (gender, ELL status, special education status, race, and FRLP)
	Diagnostic screenings/ formative assessments	What are the skill levels across all groups and within groups (gender, race, and FRLP)? What percentage of students fall into each level of risk by groups (gender, race, and FRLP)? How have participating students moved? What is the wellness of intervention capacity and implementation?	DIBELS (example)	Number of students within each level of risk overall and by gender, ELL status, special education status, race and FRLP Percentage of students within each level moved up or down

Month	Practice/Process Events	Critical Process/Practice Questions	Available Data	Types of Analysis
MAY	School attendance report	What is the daily attendance for all groups? Are there specific groups of students missing 1–3 days, and more than 4 days? How is tardiness marked by staff?	Attendance	Attendance patterns include tardiness and absences overall and by gender, ELL status, special education status, race, and FRLP
	Course grades	What is the average grade across all groups (gender, race, and FRLP)? What is the average grade by classroom and content area?	Semester grades	Number and percentage of students getting As and Bs, Cs and Ds, and Fs Average grades by classroom and content overall and by gender, ELL status, special education status, race, and FRLP
	Disciplinary referrals	What are the rates of disciplinary referrals? What are the average types of "offenses"? What are the interventions for these "offenses"? What are the location and time of day of "offenses"? Who is doing the referring?	Disciplinary referrals	Number of students referred for discipline Percentage of students referred for discipline by groups (gender, ELL status, special education status, race and FRLP)

Data Process Template

	How many students are challenged this period? (*Note:* More than 15%–20% of students experiencing attendance, behavioral, and/or achievement issues require a closer look at core attendance, behavioral, and academic support program)	What was the wellness of the process this period? (E.g., was there a new attendance policy in place? Were teachers spending more time doing test prep this month? Was there a new behavioral reward system in place, if so, did everyone do it consistently?)
Attendance Data		
Behavioral Data		
Achievement Data		

Copyright © 2017 by Corwin. All rights reserved. Reprinted from *Solving Disproportionality and Achieving Equity: A Leader's Guide to Using Data to Change Hearts and Minds* by Edward Fergus. Thousand Oaks, CA: Corwin, www.corwin.com. Reproduction authorized only for the local school site or nonprofit organization that has purchased this book.

Next Steps for [INSERT MONTH] _____

Implementation (Tasks and activities needed to make process and practice improvements)				
Identify Specific Strategies to Improve	Plans for Completing Tasks and Activities (i.e., the steps school will take to implement)	Staff Responsible for Tasks and Activities	Timeline for Completion of Tasks and Activities	Start and End Dates

Copyright © 2017 by Corwin. All rights reserved. Reprinted from *Solving Disproportionality and Achieving Equity: A Leader's Guide to Using Data to Change Hearts and Minds* by Edward Fergus. Thousand Oaks, CA: Corwin, www.corwin.com. Reproduction authorized only for the local school site or nonprofit organization that has purchased this book.

ADDITIONAL EQUITY EXAMINATIONS

Course grades along with other outcomes (e.g., attendance, credit accumulation) appear to operate as predictors of high school graduation. Thus I have developed this workbook as a means to assist school districts conduct a RCA of their course grade outcomes in relation to academic support systems. A core outcome analysis framework is to examine disproportionate representation. Disproportionality is the overrepresentation of a specific group relative to the presence of this group in the overall student population, and/or the underrepresentation of a specific group in accessing intervention services, resources, programs, rigorous curriculum and instruction relative to the presence of this group in the overall student population. At the core of our analysis framework is to examine disproportionate representation. This involves conducting specific analyses, such as risk index, composition analysis, and/or relative risk ratio. The workbook provides practitioners an opportunity to reflect on the outcomes, consider pertinent practice and policy areas, conduct specific analyses of specific policy and practice areas, identify gaps in practice and policy, and define specific remedies for the identified gaps.

Course Grade Worksheets

These worksheets are designed to give a layered analysis of course grade data. By using several formulas to look at course grade data, users of these worksheets are able to generate a multiperspective view of course grade data, necessary to identify achievement underperformance and track its growth or reduction within a district or school.

Analysis 1: Risk of Students Passing and Failing Courses by Race/Ethnicity

1. Observed Risk Indexes Rate by Race/Ethnicity of Passing 9th Grade English Language Arts

	Black	Hispanic	White	Asian	Total
A. Observed Course Grades	# receive As, Bs, and Cs	# receive As, Bs, and Cs	# receive As, Bs, and Cs	# receive As, Bs, and Cs	# Total receive As, Bs, and Cs
B. Total Enrolled	# enrolled	# enrolled	# enrolled	# enrolled	Total # enrolled
C. Risk Index	$A/B \times 100$	$A/B \times 100$	$A/B \times 100$	$A/B \times 100$	$A/B \times 100$

2. Observed Risk Indexes Rate by Race/Ethnicity of Failing 9th Grade English Language Arts

	Black	Hispanic	White	Asian	Total
A. Observed Course Grades	# receive Ds and Fs	# receive Ds and Fs	# receive Ds and Fs	# receive Ds and Fs	Total # receive Ds and Fs
B. Total Enrolled	# enrolled	# enrolled	# enrolled	# enrolled	Total # enrolled
C. Risk Index	A/B × 100	A/B × 100	A/B × 100	A/B × 100	A/B × 100

3. Observed Risk Indexes Rate by Race/Ethnicity of Passing 9th Grade Math

	Black	Hispanic	White	Asian	Total
A. Observed Course Grades	# receive As, Bs, and Cs	# receive As, Bs, and Cs	# receive As, Bs, and Cs	# receive As, Bs, and Cs	# Total receive As, Bs, and Cs
B. Total Enrolled	# enrolled	# enrolled	# enrolled	# enrolled	Total # enrolled
C. Risk Index	A/B × 100	A/B × 100	A/B × 100	A/B × 100	A/B × 100

4. Observed Risk Indexes Rate by Race/Ethnicity of Failing 9th Grade Math

	Black	Hispanic	White	Asian	Total
A. Observed Course Grades	# receive Ds and Fs	# receive Ds and Fs	# receive Ds and Fs	# receive Ds and Fs	Total # receive Ds and Fs
B. Total Enrolled	# enrolled	# enrolled	# enrolled	# enrolled	Total # enrolled
C. Risk Index	A/B × 100	A/B × 100	A/B × 100	A/B × 100	A/B × 100

Analysis 2: Risk of Students Passing and Failing Courses by Gender

5. Observed Risk Indexes Rate by Gender of Passing 9th Grade English Language Arts

	Male	Female	Total
A. Observed Course Grades	# receive As, Bs, and Cs	# receive As, Bs, and Cs	# Total receive As, Bs, and Cs
B. Total Enrolled	# enrolled	# enrolled	Total # enrolled
C. Risk Index	A/B × 100	A/B × 100	A/B × 100

6. Observed Risk Indexes Rate by Gender of Failing 9th Grade English Language Arts

	Male	Female	Total
A. Observed Course Grades	# receive Ds and Fs	# receive Ds and Fs	Total # receive Ds and Fs
B. Total Enrolled	# enrolled	# enrolled	Total # enrolled
C. Risk Index	A/B × 100	A/B × 100	A/B × 100

7. Observed Risk Indexes Rate by Gender of Passing 9th Grade Math

	Male	Female	Total
A. Observed Course Grades	# receive As, Bs, and Cs	# receive As, Bs, and Cs	# Total receive As, Bs, and Cs
B. Total Enrolled	# enrolled	# enrolled	Total # enrolled
C. Risk Index	A/B × 100	A/B × 100	A/B × 100

8. Observed Risk Indexes Rate by Gender of Failing 9th Grade Math

	Male	Female	Total
A. Observed Course Grades	# receive Ds and Fs	# receive Ds and Fs	Total # receive Ds and Fs
B. Total Enrolled	# enrolled	# enrolled	Total # enrolled
C. Risk Index	A/B × 100	A/B × 100	A/B × 100

Analysis 3: Risk of Students Passing and Failing Courses by ELL Status

9. Observed Risk Indexes Rate by ELL Status of Passing 9th Grade English Language Arts

	ELL	Non-ELL	Total
A. Observed Course Grades	# receive As, Bs, and Cs	# receive As, Bs, and Cs	# Total receive As, Bs, and Cs
B. Total Enrolled	# enrolled	# enrolled	Total # enrolled
C. Risk Index	A/B × 100	A/B × 100	A/B × 100

10. Observed Risk Indexes Rate by ELL Status of Failing 9th Grade English Language Arts

	Male	Female	Total
A. Observed Course Grades	# receive Ds and Fs	# receive Ds and Fs	Total # receive Ds and Fs
B. Total Enrolled	# enrolled	# enrolled	Total # enrolled
C. Risk Index	A/B × 100	A/B × 100	A/B × 100

11. Observed Risk Indexes Rate by ELL Status of Passing 9th Grade Math

	Male	Female	Total
A. Observed Course Grades	# receive As, Bs, and Cs	# receive As, Bs, and Cs	# Total receive As, Bs, and Cs
B. Total Enrolled	# enrolled	# enrolled	Total # enrolled
C. Risk Index	A/B × 100	A/B × 100	A/B × 100

12. Observed Risk Indexes Rate by ELL Status of Failing 9th Grade Math

	Male	Female	Total
A. Observed Course Grades	# receive Ds and Fs	# receive Ds and Fs	Total # receive Ds and Fs
B. Total Enrolled	# enrolled	# enrolled	Total # enrolled
C. Risk Index	A/B × 100	A/B × 100	A/B × 100

Reflection

Data Tool Patterns	Identify Group(s)	Designation
Risk index of receiving As, Bs, and Cs is higher than 80%.		Appropriate Passing Rates
Risk index of receiving As, Bs, and Cs is less than 80%.		Concern in Passing Rates
Risk index of receiving Ds and Fs is higher than 20%.		Inappropriate Failure Rates

Gradebook Audit

The purpose of this monthly grade book audit template is to provide a starting point for asking equity questions during the data analysis process. Schools and districts need to develop data systems, as well as conduct analyses of these data. However, there is little guidance as to *what* questions to ask of data as well as *what to do* with the answers. The intent with this monthly grade book audit is to look inside the process of grading and the distribution of learning opportunities. More specifically, this analysis provides an instructional perspective on whether students with a range of learning needs are getting varied, robust, and timely opportunities to learn new content and skills as well as demonstrate them in a myriad of formats. Additionally, our perspective within this monthly grade book audit includes an understanding that there are various points in the educational process in which racial/ethnic minority, low-income, and linguistically diverse populations are not receiving an equitable opportunity; thus, the analysis questions that are posed are not only to monitor academic outcomes early enough, but also as an early warning or monitoring as to whether the educational process is equitable and accessible.

Infrastructure and Process

1. Begin with building level leadership to conduct monthly data analysis of this level. The intention of this process to assist in guiding instructional management decisions.

2. Work with your data personnel to ascertain the following: the availability of data, the work involved in generating reports on these variables, the quality of the data entry, the consistency of data entry, etc.

3. The intent of the process is to assist your team to consistently understand the nature of student progress and its relationship to the wellness of instructional improvement implementation.

4. Define the nature of the grade audit. Identify the semester/quarter, the 4-week period, the content, and grade levels of focus.

Teacher: _____ or Content area focus[4]: _____

Semester/Quarter:_____ or 4-week period: _____

Grade-level focus: _____

	All Students	White Students	Black Students	Latino Students	Asian Students	Native American Students
Assessments 1. **Total number of assessments**						
2. **Total number of students**						
3. **Average assessment grade** • **Assessment 1 average** • **Assessment 2 average** • **Assessment 3 average** • **Assessment 4 average** *Note:* **Calculation of average is total score of assessments among all students divided by total number of students.**						

---

[4] Depending on the size of the middle or high school, being able to conduct a grade book audit for all grade levels and content areas may be difficult. Focusing on a specific content area and grade level may be more manageable.

	All Students	White Students	Black Students	Latino Students	Asian Students	Native American Students
Classwork 1. **Total number of classwork assignments**						
2. **Total number of students**						
3. **Average classwork assignment grade** • **Assignment 1 average** • **Assignment 2 average** • **Assignment 3 average** • **Assignment 4 average** • **Assignment 5 average** • **Assignment 6 average** • **Assignment 7 average** • **Assignment 8 average** *Note:* **Calculation of average is total score of assessments among all students divided by total number of students.**						

	All Students	White Students	Black Students	Latino Students	Asian Students	Native American Students
Homework 1. Total number of homework assignments						
2. Total number of students						
3. Average homework assignment grade • Assignment 1 average • Assignment 2 average • Assignment 3 average • Assignment 4 average • Assignment 5 average • Assignment 6 average • Assignment 7 average • Assignment 8 average *Note:* Calculation of average is total score of assessments among all students divided by total number of students.						

	All Students	White Students	Black Students	Latino Students	Asian Students	Native American Students
Participation 1. **Total number of participation activities/ entries**						
2. **Total number of students**						
3. **Average participation activity/entry grade** • **Activity/entry 1 average** • **Activity/entry 2 average** • **Activity/entry 3 average** • **Activity/entry 4 average** • **Activity/entry 5 average** • **Activity/entry 6 average** • **Activity/entry 7 average** • **Activity/entry 8 average** *Note:* **Calculation of average is total score of assessments among all students divided by total number of students.**						

	All Students	White Students	Black Students	Latino Students	Asian Students	Native American Students
Overall passing rate						
1. Number of As						
2. Number of Bs						
3. Number of Cs						
4. Number of Ds						
5. Number of Fs						
Note: **If applicable, the overall passing rate analysis can also be conducted by other demographic groups (e.g., lunch status, gender, language status)**						

Copyright © 2017 by Corwin. All rights reserved. Reprinted from *Solving Disproportionality and Achieving Equity: A Leader's Guide to Using Data to Change Hearts and Minds* by Edward Fergus. Thousand Oaks, CA: Corwin, www.corwin.com. Reproduction authorized only for the local school site or nonprofit organization that has purchased this book.

Aggregate Worksheet

On this worksheet, compile the overall patterns from the previous worksheets conducted for each teacher. The intention of this worksheet is to be able to see all the patterns across a grade level and/or content area.

	[Teacher Name]	[Teacher Name]	[Teacher Name]
Analysis Consideration **What are the patterns that you notice? Below are possible things to look for:** • **Are students receiving high percentage points in classwork/ homework and participation but failing assessments?** • **Is there an even distribution of grades?** • **Are students getting enough opportunities to demonstrate learning growth?** • **What learning activities (assessments, participation, classwork, and/or homework) are influencing overall pasting rates?**			
Overall Action Steps 1. **Consider the professional development that is needed.** 2. **Consider conducting a grade-level or content-level meeting about the results and defining next steps.** 3. **Consider providing weekly support for teachers on how to construct additional assignments during a week's lesson plan.** 4. **Define the weekly changes expected for the upcoming 4 weeks.**			

Copyright © 2017 by Corwin. All rights reserved. Reprinted from *Solving Disproportionality and Achieving Equity: A Leader's Guide to Using Data to Change Hearts and Minds* by Edward Fergus. Thousand Oaks, CA: Corwin, www.corwin.com. Reproduction authorized only for the local school site or nonprofit organization that has purchased this book.

Chapter 5

Building an Equity Belief School Climate

Over the many years of working with school districts to develop, implement, and monitor an equity perspective and pedagogical lens, there is nothing more difficult than reformulating the beliefs or worldviews of individuals. Before school/district leaders embark on reformulating these beliefs, they need to know why these bias-based beliefs matter and how they operate.

First, as described in Chapter 2, the various forms of bias-based beliefs are powerful worldviews that assist individuals in making sense of the world. To change these beliefs or worldviews, we must have a replacement belief. Trying to argue that a deficit or colorblind belief keeps an individual blind is an undeveloped approach because we have to fundamentally understand that there needs to be a replacement belief that an individual can use to drive his or her thinking. For instance, it's a deficit belief that allows for individuals to walk by a homeless person who holds a sign "I'm homeless, please help" and rationalize the person's condition is a result of self-doing instead of viewing that this individual's condition requires more structural support to prevent it from happening. This belief in particular, as discussed in Chapter 2, is based on an individualistic perspective of mobility according to which "we make our own future." Another example of deficit thinking can be found when some practitioners criticize youth that "sag" their pants (wear pants below the waistline, thus exposing underwear). The deficit view is seeing such youth culture behavior as a signal of not being serious about the schooling process. A replacement belief of deficit thinking would be an asset-based view that this is an expression of youth culture similar to hippie clothing during the 1970s. The purpose of a replacement belief is to recognize that although each person makes behavioral decisions based on available information and perspectives on a situation, youth are in multiple stages of development, and an assets-based belief is a better place to scaffold into improvement.

A second component to understand about undoing these bias-based beliefs is that they are not static. They maintain levels of flexibility in which individuals will suspend their bias-based beliefs when they can detect an "undeserving" condition. Herbert Gans (1996) argues that in the United States, poor people are divided into simplistic camps of "deserving" and "undeserving" poor. In the example about the homeless person, many individuals would render that person as deserving poor if they were male and/or a Black, Latino, and/or Native American. However, if the homeless person held a sign that stated, "I'm an Iraq War Veteran and I am homeless," the bias-based belief would be suspended, or there would be an exception made, because there is a perception that people who served in military and are veterans are undeserving of being homeless.

As a result of these various dynamics about bias-based beliefs, its imperative leaders know how to lead and manage these conversations in a constructive manner. There are several Leading Equity Competencies that leaders need to practice and/or be aware of: (1) knowing how race dialogues, specifically, can be co-opted; and (2) knowing how to manage the comfortable and uncomfortable zones for individuals.

LEADING EQUITY COMPETENCY 1: KNOW HOW TO MANAGE RACE DIALOGUES

Derald Wing Sue (2013), in a study of classroom dialogues on race, identifies three separate conversation protocols that get in the way of productive race conversations—politeness, academic, and colorblindness. Each protocol operates differently with the end goal of managing these dialogues in such a way that White practitioners do not experience guilt or fragility (DiAngelo, 2011). The politeness protocol refers to the societal expectation that certain topics (for example, religion, money, and race) should be avoided in "mixed" company. The politeness protocol helps to manage race dialogues from being discussed and/or being carried forward by many participants in any conversation. The second protocol is academic. This protocol governs our conversation by insisting that emotions are omitted from any race dialogue; it's the old adage "let's not get emotional," or "can we just keep it to the facts without emotion." Conversations about race necessitate emotions to be expressed to a certain extent because it is another form of oppression to silence or have marginalized groups to share their narrative without emotions; experiences of marginalization leave an individual with emotional scars. And the third protocol is colorblindness. This protocol refers to the universalizing of marginalization; this is often heard in the form of "I grew poor and White with Black people, so I understand," or "I experience similar marginalization because I am gay." The difficulty of such dialogue is twofold: (1) It creates an "oppression Olympics" conversation that stalls our ability to discuss each form of oppression; and (2) the approach of universalizing oppression makes race a null or unimportant conversation point.

Sue (2013) offers the following strategies for managing these conversation protocols:

- Facilitators must understand themselves as racial and cultural beings, which includes recognizing their own values, biases, and assumptions.
- Facilitators show openness and ability to acknowledge and validate discussions of feelings.
- Facilitators know how to manage the process of race dialogue and not control the content.
- Facilitators are able to use exercises and assignments to elicit race dialogues.
- Facilitators teach others how to manage racial blunders.

LEADING EQUITY COMPETENCY 2: KNOW HOW TO MANAGE THE COMFORTABLE AND UNCOMFORTABLE TENSIONS OF LEARNING AND PRACTICE

Pollock, Deckman, Mira, and Shalaby (2010) identify a very compelling question that emerges among teachers during race dialogues—*But what can I do?* This question not only shows tensions regarding the content of race and racism, but more importantly, it raises three tensions that Pollock et al. (2010) identify as interlocked with this question. These three tensions are the following: personal, structural, and strategies. In various trainings, I use these tensions as a way for exploring what practitioners expect to occur during an equity session.

The personal tension of *what can **I** do* involves the personal inquiry and readiness regarding race and racism, such as, how often do I engage with others different than myself, what is my level of comfort with others different than myself, what is my racial memory, what are the cultural artifacts that define myself, who are my affinity groups, etc. The structural tension of *what **can** I do* involves an inquiry into the individual's power and agency within specified structural conditions, such as segregation, oppression, racism, etc. This tension is where practitioners feel goals of equity are insurmountable because these structural conditions are beyond the scope and realm of the individual. And the final tension is the strategies tension of *what can I **do*** which involves being able to articulate notions of equity into actionable activities within classrooms and school environments.

Pollock et al. (2010) offers the following strategies for managing these conversation tensions:

- Facilitators should not aim to resolve the tensions, but rather keep them active. The absence of these tensions could result in simplistic solutions to complex race issues.

- Facilitators should encourage practitioners to consider all tensions simultaneously while trying to resolve race issues.
- Facilitators should continuously ask the question, "So how could we apply this?" while exploring race issues.

STAGE 1 ACTIVITIES: BUILDING UNIVERSAL EQUITY PRINCIPLES

Building of a universalizing message of equity that is focused on creating new futures versus filling gaps can be an arduous process for a variety of reasons. First, any process in which consensus is necessary requires leaders who are comfortable with listening to everyone's perspective and harnessing it into a decision. Thomas Hoerr (2005) argues that leaders need to know when to understand that some decisions are "your decision, our decision or my decision." Developing a universal message of equity is something that is our decision!

Closely connected to this concept of decision making are two necessary capacities: (1) managing conversations about equitable outcomes and (2) having a clarity of your own understanding of how issues of racism, sexism, heteronormative expectations, ableism, and other oppressive social structures operate. The first capacity relates to the exposure to equity-based conversations. It is difficult to know how a conversation regarding a specific equity issue will unfold if you've never done it or because you are not clear as to what makes it a problem or, much less, how to resolve it. For example, during a data-dive session with a district-level team of a large urban school system (over 80,000 students), we were looking at data on disproportionality patterns in suspension, special education, and gifted programs, and an assistant superintendent shared the level of uncomfortableness when discussing subgroups. More specifically, the assistant superintendent stated feeling uncomfortable saying "Black" because this individual grew up being told not to use that term or being shunned when describing someone as Black. This example shows the interaction between these two capacities—managing equity dialogue and comfort with understanding oppression structures. As a response to dealing with these two capacity issues, I paused our data dive and focused on doing two things. First, underscoring the importance of being comfortable when discussing race. I had the team members saying "Black" about three or four times; the intention was to have them begin dismissing the idea that it is impolite to use race descriptors. As Sue (2013) discusses, it is such a protocol that gets in the way

Sample Equity Principles

1. Create an additive (not subtractive or deficit-oriented), welcoming, inclusive, and *safe school environment.*

2. Create and implement an *equitable recruitment and hiring model* that ensures the personnel who reflects our community demographics is hired.

3. Identify and examine critical disparities in our educational system to ensure that *opportunities and supports exist for high achievement by each and every student* regardless of special needs, race, ethnicity, or financial status.

4. Assist in identifying teaching and learning strategies and approaches that help to raise student achievement for *all* students, *in particular those students of color* who may need additional assistance.

5. Recommend and promote policies, practices, and programs that enhance, encourage, and foster effective student participation in a diverse and inclusive community.

of being able to lead and manage race dialogues. Second, I had the team discuss what the discomfort in leading race dialogues suggests to other practitioners, or what I like to call, "not saying race says it all!" It was the latter part of the dialogue that elicited constructive thinking and role-playing among this district-level team on how they could support each other in leading and managing equity-driven work.

Overall, research demonstrates that the work leaders need to do for engaging in this can involve storied selves that reflect personal experiences (Boske, 2015), participating in peer collaborative groups in order to practice with others (Winkelman, 2012), understanding of social structures and its unique impact on specific groups (e.g., English emergent students, Native American students; Wiemelt & Welton, 2015), and balancing personal with professional ethics and moral imperatives in framing equity (Maxwell, Locke, & Scheurich, 2014; McClellan & Casey, 2015; Pollack & Zirkel, 2013; Rivera-McCutchen, 2014; Theohanis, 2008). This does not mean that leaders need to know about all oppressive social structures. However, they should have a level of acceptance in feeling uncomfortable when participating in these conversations.

The following activities utilize a consensus-building approach to develop a universal message of equity.

Activity 1.1: Building Common Definitions of Educational Equity

Time Required: 1 hour 30 minutes

Materials Required: Definitions of Educational Equity Worksheet (see Appendix 4); pencils or pens; newsprint or chart paper; markers

Purpose: To have practitioners provide their own definitions of educational equity, this activity allows them to react to various definitions. Additionally, this activity provides an opportunity for biased views (i.e., deficit thinking, colorblindness, and poverty disciplining) to emerge, and be discussed and potentially replaced.

Process: Each practitioner receives the Definitions of Educational Equity Worksheet and is given about 2–5 minutes to write down his or her reactions to various definitions. The intent of providing different definitions is to highlight the various dimensions of equity (i.e., culture, interaction, curriculum, outcome) and how each author has explored these concepts. After reading the definitions and writing down their reactions, each practitioner should pair up with someone else and discuss his or her reactions for 12–15 minutes. Specifically, the discussion should focus on answering two questions: (1) How do these definitions add to my own understanding of educational equity; and (2) what are the tensions in trying to achieve these forms of educational equity?

After the small-group discussion, the facilitator asks for volunteer pairs to share their conversation with the larger group; again, the discussion should focus on the two questions. This part of the exercise can last between 15 and 30 minutes, depending on group dynamics. The following are samples of some of the dynamics that may emerge: (1) practitioners getting stuck on terminology; (2) practitioners discussing the tension of not being able to please everyone; (3) practitioners worried about having to know about all cultural groups; (4) practitioners worried that educational equity prevents holding students accountable for behaviors they consider nonconducive for educational success; and (5) practitioners excited about moving in the direction of attaining educational equity, but unsure of where to start.

As homework or scaffold for the next session, practitioners should identify at least one area of their district, school, and/or classroom practice (e.g., curriculum, lesson planning, cooperative grouping, gifted/AP/honors class enrollment, homework assignments, classroom management, academic/behavioral interventions process, interpretation of assessment data, grade book distribution of assignments) and identify how practice would change in applying each definition. Practitioners should use the Applying Definitions of Educational Equity worksheets (see Appendixes 5 and 6) to capture the practice and outline how the practice would change.

Activity 1.2: Practicing Applying Definitions of Educational Equity

Time Required: 1 hour 30 minutes

Materials Required: Applying Definitions of Educational Equity (see Appendix 5); Applying Definitions of Educational Equity: Homework Worksheet (see Appendix 6); pencils or pens; newsprint or chart paper; markers

Purpose: Practitioners apply definitions of educational equity. In order to start building a consensus on educational equity, this activity represents an opportunity to connect relevant concepts of equity. Additionally, these activities provide an opportunity for biased views (i.e., deficit thinking, colorblindness, and poverty disciplining) to emerge, and be discussed and potentially replaced.

Preworkshop Work: Remind practitioners about completing Applying Definitions of Educational Equity: Homework Worksheet. Facilitator should create table tents or sheets of paper displaying the following categories: curriculum, academic/behavioral intervention referral process, gifted/AP/honors referral and enrollment, instructional strategies, classroom management, assessment, and classroom climate/environment. These table tents or sheets of paper should be placed on random tables in the professional development space.

Process: Each practitioner should arrive to professional development session with the Applying Definitions of Educational Equity: Homework Worksheet (see Appendix 6) completed. Facilitator instructs practitioners to identify the one practice they focused on and take a seat at the appropriate table. For example, if a practitioner selected his or her grading policy/practice, then he or she should sit at the table labeled "assessments." Ideally, facilitator wants to make sure there are not more than five or six practitioners per table. Once groups are formed, facilitators shall instruct practitioners to share out with each other: (1) how they perceived their practice changing as result of equity definition; and (2) what is the potential outcome of such a change. Allow groups about 20–30 minutes to discuss.

After small-group conversation, sample groups should share out some of the highlights discussed that are related to the two questions posed. This should take about 15–30 minutes. Afterward, facilitator shall engage group in another exercise in which practitioners will be able to apply concepts of equity. Facilitator shall provide each practitioner with the Applying Definitions of Educational Equity handout (see Appendix 5). Each practitioner shall examine the pictures and answer the questions in the table. This should take about 5–8 minutes. Then facilitator allows practitioners to share their answers in groups of four to five. This small-group component should take about 15–20 minutes. After small-group conversation, sample groups should share out some of the highlights discussed in their groups related to the questions posed. This should take about 15–30 minutes. Upon completion of large-group share out, facilitator can give practitioner readings (see Equity Resources for Curricular, Culture/Climate, and Instruction, Appendix 23) as homework for the next session, which focuses on developing schoolwide equity principles.

Activity 1.3: Creating Schoolwide Equity Principles

Time Required: 1 hour 30 minutes

Materials Required: Building Our Universal Equity Principles Worksheet (see Appendix 7)

Purpose: Practitioners define schoolwide principles of educational equity. This activity should include a significant group discussion that will lead to highlighting of five core principles.

Process: Each practitioner receives the Building Our Universal Equity Principles Worksheet along with a writing instrument. The worksheet contains four boxes—individual, pair, quad, and octet. Each practitioner takes about 5–7 minutes to answer the following question in the box labeled *individual*: What are the five ideas/concepts that define educational equity for you? Then the practitioner pairs up with another practitioner to share the five ideas/concepts for about 8–10 minutes. The paired group should discuss why these five ideas/concepts are important in their definition of

Garden Hills Elementary School, Champaign Unit 4, Illinois; 2013–2014 school year; Principal Cheryl Camacho-Lewis, Assistant Principal Delores Lloyd

- Education is a civil right supported through a collective commitment to social justice and equity.
- Every child deserves to go to school in a healthy, safe, engaging, supportive, and challenging environment.
- Teaching school-dependent children is hard but rewarding work that requires a growth mindset, grit, perseverance, and resiliency.
- We serve students in Grades K–5; nothing is set in stone and their potential is unlimited. No child should be written off, especially not before their 13th year of life. We should do everything that we can to highlight strengths and possibility to our children and their families.

educational equity. The pair should write down in the pair box on the worksheet the common concepts. The intention of this step is to assist the practitioner to begin articulating why these five concepts matter, where do they come from, and how do they affect their behavior toward achieving educational equity. Then the practitioner pair moves into a quad (group of four) and discuss again their five concepts of educational equity; this step should last 15–20 minutes. The quad should write down the common concepts. Again, this group should articulate why these five concepts matter, where do they come from, and how do they affect their behavior toward achieving educational equity. Finally, the practitioner quad moves into an octet (group of eight) with a focus on sharing their five concepts in order to arrive at consensus about which five concepts are critically important and why; this step should last 20–25 minutes. At the beginning of the octet step, each group should have a large sheet of paper and markers to write down the final five concepts they have agreed on.

Once each octet group has completed writing down their final five concepts, each individual would've had an opportunity to discuss his or her personal and professional understandings of educational equity, engage in dialogue with others that may share or not understandings of educational equity, and reach consensus on educational equity. Each octet group should take about 5–10 minutes to share out with the large group and post their large sheet of paper on a blank wall. At the end of this session, there typically are common principles that emerge, and as leader, it will be important to review these principles against the definitions of educational equity worksheet. At the end of these exercises, the school staff should have working definitions of educational equity and be engaged in a vigorous conversation that would lead to development of universal principles of educational equity. These principles should be utilized as anchors for examining the manner in which educational practices and processes are developed, implemented, monitored, and identified as effective.

Postworkshop Activity: In order to ensure the school staff are moving toward equity principles that challenge bias-based beliefs, there needs to be an assessment of these principles. I encourage leaders to establish an ad hoc equity committee that will take a closer look at these principles. The closer look will involve: (1) examining the principles against the definitions found on the Definitions of Educational Equity Worksheet; and (2) utilize the checklist on the following page to ascertain whether these principles enhance, detract, or plateau the school's desired state of minimizing disproportionality and creating educational equity practices and outcomes.

Equity Team: Educational Equity Check-In

Educational Equity Check-In: Consider the following components and assess the wellness of Stage 1 activities on defining educational equity.

	Notes
1. Equity needs to contain at least three components.	
a. **Numerical framing of equity**—*name the outcome to be changed; for example, reduce disproportionate representation by at least 25%; or increase enrollment of racial/ethnic minority student populations in gifted, AP/honors courses.*	
b. **Social justice framing of equity**—*name the access and opportunity to achieve and/or change; for example, remove the use of suspension as an intervention and implement with fidelity supports for behavior modification; or reduce utilization of teacher recommendation for gifted and AP/honors enrollment and implement with fidelity supports for academic acceleration in intervention programming.*	
c. **Culture and Belief Environment of equity**—*name and reduce the beliefs that frame and impact perceptions of cognitive and behavioral abilities; for example, our school environment will remove deficit framing of students behavior and focus on using empowering language of strengths and potential; or our school climate and culture will acknowledge that colorblindness ignores the strengths found in social identities, and will work toward supporting the affirmative development of social identities.*	
2. Do these principles harness the concepts of educational equity outlined in the Definitions of Educational Equity Worksheet?	
3. Is there a balance of educational equity principles that are geared toward changing adult practice and system processes?	
4. Do these principles focus on "fixing" students via language such as "cultivate students to be studious" or "champions of their own future"?	

Copyright © 2017 by Corwin. All rights reserved. Reprinted from *Solving Disproportionality and Achieving Equity: A Leader's Guide to Using Data to Change Hearts and Minds* by Edward Fergus. Thousand Oaks, CA: Corwin, www.corwin.com. Reproduction authorized only for the local school site or nonprofit organization that has purchased this book.

STAGE 2 ACTIVITIES: MONTHLY OR QUARTERLY SESSIONS ON BIAS-BASED BELIEFS

School and district leaders often hire consultants to do certain types of "diversity" or equity trainings. Although I consider these professional development activities as important "jumpstarts" for building an equitable school or district system, there is typically a loss of traction. The loss generally occurs because there is no specific strategy that would make equity to become a new ethos—that is, *replace bias-based beliefs*. The following activities are intended to be the "traction" in between your "diversity" jumpstarts. Additionally, these activities provide opportunities for showcasing the limitations of bias-based beliefs and developing a new set of beliefs that coincide with the equity principles developed during Stage 1 Activities.

Deficit Thinking

As described in Chapter 2, deficit thinking is an ideology used to explain academic performance and at times, cognitive abilities as a result of deficiencies within a cultural group. And more importantly, this ideology discounts the role of systemic issues via language such as "discrimination was outlawed decades ago, how could it still have an impact," "shouldn't they be responsible for their own behavior," "they need to learn the language of power if they want to fit in," and "we can't keep accommodating them." The following activities are intended to provide an opportunity for practitioners to understand the limitations and impact of deficit thinking on their students and their own professional and personalized experiences.

Activity 2.1a: Unpacking the Deficit-Thinking Elephant

Time Required: 1 hour 30 minutes

Materials Required: Shifting Deficit-Thinking Worksheet (see Appendix 8)

Purpose: Allow practitioners consider how deficit thinking as an ideology relies on consistently framing the abilities and behaviors of low-income and racial/ethnic minority students with a deficit orientation.

Process: Each practitioner will receive the Shifting Deficit-Thinking Worksheet and get into a small group (two to four individuals). The group will spend about 15–20 minutes discussing the first two columns of worksheet—the deficit thinking phrases and how to identify deficit trait(s). The purpose of this first part of the activity is (1) recognizing commonly stated deficit-based thoughts, and (2) defining how these statements engender a deficit trait. Depending on prior knowledge and exposure of the group to the concept, the facilitator may need to walk through several of the statements as a large group to help practitioners recognize statements as deficit thinking and identify the deficit traits. An additional tool that can be shared with the group is the Definition Flashcards (see Appendix 10); this tool can be used as a quick reminder for understanding and identifying deficit thinking.

After the small-group exercise, allow for two small groups to combine together and discuss their understanding of deficit thinking. The intention of this additional small-group debrief is to allow practitioners to discuss with their colleagues these complex concepts and listen to other beliefs. Although practitioners are often emotionally exhausted after sessions like these, it is imperative that the leaders provide various opportunities for staff to continue this excavation of beliefs through different types of homework or extending learning opportunities. The following are examples I have seen school leaders provide for their staff:

- **Three-by-ten dialogue:** Practitioner identifies a student or two he or she continuously refers for behavioral issues and spends 3 minutes for 10 consecutive days asking these students about their interests, things they do after school, and dreams. Such a socioemotional development activity allows practitioners to learn more about the child they may only view as a "problem."
- **Seeing the everyday deficit language:** Practitioners chose during the course of a 2-week period a space where they will sit for about 15 minutes and listen for language used by adults when interacting with children. These spaces could be a colleague's classroom, hallway, playground, cafeteria, or a combination. Practitioners should commit to at least doing this 2 times during 2 weeks and, after each encounter, document some of the language used and include the date. To maintain anonymity, the leader can create a box to anonymously insert observations and document deficit language. This activity is intended to assist practitioners listening for deficit-coded language.

Activity 2.1b: Unpacking the Deficit-Thinking Elephant—Survey Activity

Time Required: 1 hour 30 minutes

Materials Required: Shifting Deficit-Thinking Survey Worksheet (see Appendix 9)

Purpose: Allow practitioners consider how deficit thinking as an ideology relies on consistently framing the abilities and behaviors of low-income and racial/ethnic minority students with a deficit orientation.

Process: Each practitioner will receive the Shifting Deficit-Thinking Survey Worksheet and respond to each statement with *agree, neutral,* or *disagree.* Give practitioners about 5–8 minutes to complete the survey and remind them that it is anonymous. Once practitioners complete the survey, have them fold it at least 2 times and place it on a table at the center or front of the room. Once all folded surveys are on the table, facilitator should move around folded surveys to make sure they are mixed up. Then, ask each practitioner to select a sheet of paper.

Facilitator should identify three sections of the room—*agree, neutral,* or *disagree.* Ask each practitioner to open their sheet of paper. The facilitator shall read each statement and allow practitioners to move around the room to the respective corners—agree, neutral, or disagree. Pause in between each statement to allow practitioners to look around and absorb the various perspectives on deficit thoughts. Once the facilitator finishes reading each statement, allow practitioners to pair up and briefly discuss their initial reactions to the various statements. After 5 minutes of paired discussion, facilitator should lead a large group conversation using the following questions—*what are some of the topics discussed in your paired group, what statement stood out to you (positive and negative), and what are some other deficit thoughts you hear about racial/ethnic minority or low-income students?*

Although practitioners often are emotionally exhausted after sessions like these, it is imperative the leader provide various opportunities for staff to continue this excavation of beliefs through various types of homework or extending learning opportunities. The following are examples I have seen school leaders provide for their staff:

- **Three-by-ten dialogue:** Practitioner identifies a student or two he or she continuously refers for behavioral issues and spends 3 minutes for 10 consecutive days asking these students about their interests, things they do after school, and dreams. Such a socioemotional development activity allows practitioners to learn more about the child they may only view as a "problem."
- **Seeing the everyday deficit language:** Practitioners chose during the course of a 2-week period a space where they will sit for about 15 minutes and listen for language used by adults when interacting with children. These spaces could be a colleague's classroom, hallway, playground, cafeteria, or a combination. Practitioners should commit to at least doing this 2 times during 2 weeks and, after each encounter, document some of the language used and include the date. To maintain anonymity, the leader can create a box to anonymously insert observations and document deficit language. This activity is intended to assist practitioners listening for deficit-coded language.

Activity 2.2: Replacing the Deficit-Thinking Elephant

Time Required: 1 hour 30 minutes

Materials Required: Shifting Deficit-Thinking Worksheet (see Appendix 8)

Purpose: Provide practitioners an opportunity to consider how deficit thinking as an ideology relies on consistently framing the abilities and behaviors of low-income and racial/ethnic minority students with a deficit orientation.

Preworkshop Work: If facilitator provides opportunity for practitioners to do the above activity on Seeing the Everyday Deficit Language, then the information compiled in the box shall be shared at the next session.

Process: Each practitioner will receive the Shifting Deficit-Thinking Worksheet and get into a small group (two to four individuals). The group will spend about 15–20 minutes discussing the last column of the worksheet—replacing deficit-thinking phrases. The purpose of this part of the activity is to (1) consider ways in which to replace some deficit-thinking language and beliefs, and (2) practice being able to challenge each other's deficit-thinking beliefs. Depending on prior knowledge and exposure of the group to the concept, the facilitator may need to walk through several of the replacement statements as a large group to assist practitioners in recognizing how to replace these beliefs. An additional tool that can be shared with the group is the Definition Flashcards (see Appendix 10); this tool can be used as a quick reminder for understanding and identifying deficit thinking.

After the small-group exercise, allow for two small groups to combine together and discuss their replacement ides for deficit thinking. The intention of this additional small-group debrief is to allow opportunities for practitioners to discuss with their colleagues these complex concepts and explore other beliefs. This component should take about 30–40 minutes. In closing, the facilitator should request practitioners to continue spending a month listening for deficit-thinking language, documenting it, and sharing it in the anonymous box. This particular activity can serve as an opportunity for the equity team to catalogue the types and frequency of deficit-thinking language over the course of the school year, and potentially demonstrate change.

Poverty Disciplining

This form of belief, similar to deficit thinking, portrays low-income people as being at fault for persistent adverse conditions; however, poverty-disciplining bias considers changing the behavioral and psychological dispositions of these individuals as paramount to fixing their low-income condition. The practice that ensues from such a bias-based belief focuses on disciplining individuals into behaviors perceived as necessary/required for social mobility.

Activity 2.3a: Unpacking the Poverty-Disciplining Elephant

Time Required: 1 hour 30 minutes

Materials Required: Shifting Poverty-Disciplining Belief Statements Worksheet (see Appendix 11)

Purpose: Let practitioners consider how poverty disciplining as an ideology relies on consistently framing the abilities and behaviors of low-income and racial/ethnic minority students with a deficit orientation, and give them "universal" behaviors for success.

Process: Each practitioner will receive the Shifting Poverty-Disciplining Belief Statements Worksheet and get into a small group (two to four individuals). The small group will spend about 15–20 minutes discussing the first two columns of worksheet—the poverty disciplining phrases and how to identify deficit trait(s). The intention of this first part of the activity is (1) recognizing commonly stated deficit-based thoughts, and (2) defining how these statements promote a deficit trait. Depending on prior knowledge and exposure of the group to the concept, the facilitator may need to walk through several of the statements as a large group to assist practitioners in labeling statements as poverty disciplining and identifying the deficit traits. An additional tool that can be shared with the group is the Definition Flashcards (see Appendix 10); this tool can be used as a quick reminder for understanding and identifying poverty disciplining.

After the small-group exercise, allow for two small groups to combine together and discuss their understanding and identification of poverty disciplining. The intention of this additional small-group debrief is to allow opportunities for practitioners to discuss with their colleagues these complex concepts and explore other beliefs. Though often practitioners are emotionally exhausted after sessions like these, it is imperative the leader provide various opportunities for staff to continue this excavation of beliefs through various types of homework or extending learning opportunities. The following are examples I have seen school leaders provide for their staff:

- **Seeing the everyday poverty-disciplining practice:** Practitioners chose during the course of a 2-week period a space where they will sit for about 15 minutes and listen for language used by adults when interacting with children. These spaces could be a colleague's classroom, hallway, playground, cafeteria, or a combination. Practitioners should commit to at least doing this 2 times during 2 weeks and, after each encounter, document some of the language used and include the date. To maintain anonymity, the leader can create a box to anonymously insert observations and document deficit language. This activity is intended to assist practitioners listening for deficit-coded language.

Activity 2.3b: Unpacking the Poverty-Disciplining Elephant—Survey Activity

Time Required: 1 hour 30 minutes

Materials Required: Shifting Poverty-Disciplining Belief Survey Statements Worksheet (see Appendix 12)

Purpose: Let practitioners consider how poverty disciplining as an ideology relies on consistently framing the abilities and behaviors of low-income and racial/ethnic minority students with a deficit orientation.

Process: Each practitioner will receive the Shifting Poverty-Disciplining Belief Statements Survey Worksheet and respond to each statement with *agree, neutral,* or *disagree.* Give practitioners about 5–8 minutes to complete the survey and remind them that it is anonymous. Once practitioners complete the survey, have them fold it at least 2 times and place it on a table at the center or front of the room. Once all folded surveys are on the table, facilitator should move around folded surveys to make sure they are mixed up. Then, ask each practitioner to select a sheet of paper.

Facilitator should identify three sections of the room—agree, neutral, or disagree. Ask each practitioner to open their sheet of paper. The facilitator shall read each statement and allow practitioners to move around the room to the respective corners—agree, neutral, or disagree. Pause in between each statement to allow practitioners to look around and absorb the various perspectives on deficit thoughts. Once the facilitator is done reading each statement, allow practitioners to pair up and briefly discuss their initial reactions to the various statements. After 5 minutes of paired discussion, facilitator should lead a large-group conversation using the following questions—*what are some of the topics discussed in your paired group, what statement stood out to you (positive and negative), and what are some other deficit thoughts you hear about racial/ethnic minority or low-income students?*

After the small-group exercise, allow for two small groups to combine together and discuss their understanding of poverty disciplining. The intention of this additional small-group debrief is to allow opportunities for practitioners to discuss with their colleagues these complex concepts and explore other beliefs. Although practitioners are often emotionally exhausted after sessions like these, it is imperative that the leader provide various opportunities for staff to continue this excavation of beliefs through various types of homework or extending learning opportunities. The following are examples I have seen school leaders provide for their staff:

- **Seeing the everyday poverty-disciplining practice:** Practitioners chose during the course of a 2-week period a space where they will sit for about 15 minutes and listen for language used by adults when interacting with children. These spaces could be a colleague's classroom, hallway, playground, cafeteria, or a combination. Practitioners should commit to at least doing this 2 times during 2 weeks and, after each encounter, document some of the language used and include the date. To maintain anonymity, the leader can create a box to anonymously insert observations and document deficit language. This activity is intended to assist practitioners listening for deficit-coded language.

Activity 2.4: Meritocracy Line

Time Required: 1 hour 30 minutes

Materials Required: Meritocracy Line Exercise (see Appendix 13); large open room, ideally a gymnasium or cafeteria (without tables)

Purpose: The goal of the Meritocracy Line exercise is to show that class-based structures both help some individuals advance and hold other individuals back.

Process: Facilitator must ask practitioners to line up shoulder-to-shoulder in the middle of room and face the wall. The facilitator will read a statement that will let practitioners know whether to take a step forward or back. If practitioners are unsure about how to respond to the statement, they can stand still. It will take about 10–12 minutes to read all the statements and practitioners to take steps. After the last statement is read and practitioners take their final step, facilitator will ask them to look at where they started and where they are now, and to look at where their colleagues are. Facilitator will ask practitioners to get into small groups of four to six individuals who are closest to them and discuss their reactions to the exercise for about 10–20 minutes. The following are possible questions for reflection: *What statements stood out for you? Why? Were there statements in which moving forward or backward felt uncomfortable? Why? Finally, imagine your students participating in such an exercise? Where would they be on the meritocracy line?* Once the reflection time expires, facilitator should have practitioners return to a room with seating in order to lead a large-group debrief. The large-group debrief can take about 20–30 minutes and should focus on discussing the conversations of the small group. As a closing statement for practitioners, the facilitator should discuss the importance of understanding that changing behavioral and psychological dispositions of individuals experiencing poverty does not appreciate the fact of how the availability of resources changes the meritocracy available to everyone.

Activity 2.5: Schools Are Protective, Not Risk Environments

Time Required: 1 hour 30 minutes

Materials Required: Technology for streaming an online video; Dual-Axis Model of Vulnerability (see Appendix 14); Dual-Axis Model of Vulnerability Application Worksheet (see Appendix 15); newsprint; markers

Purpose: The goal of the exercise is to show that environments have the potential of creating risk and protective climates.

Process: The facilitator introduces to practitioners the need for adults to understand the complexity of environments, particularly the idea that every environment creates risk and protective climates. The facilitator asks from practitioners to share what they consider are risk factors among their students. The responses should be charted on newsprint or chart paper. Then the facilitator asks practitioners to share what they consider are protective factors among their students. The responses should be charted on newsprint or chart paper.

The facilitator provides each practitioner the Dual-Axis Model of Vulnerability (see Appendix 14) and walks through an explanation of each quadrant.

- **Top Left Quadrant—High-Risk and Low-Protective Factors:** This represents high levels of vulnerability because there are significant risks and minimal protective factors that can mitigate the effect of risks.
- **Top Right Quadrant—Low-Risk and Low-Protective Factors:** This represents masked vulnerability. It is unclear what types of difficulties may be occurring.
- **Bottom Left Quadrant—High-Risk and High-Protective Factors:** This represents low vulnerability and is considered as demonstrating resilience attributes due to the intersection of high-risk factors and high-protective factors.
- **Bottom Right Quadrant—Low-Risk and High-Protective Factors:** This represents undetermined vulnerability in which positive outcomes are predictable because of the intersection of low-risk and high-protective factors.

After explaining each quadrant, the facilitator could do one of the following:

1. Show the following video of Jose Antonio Vargas: https://youtu.be/ TJH1IKqF8PA. Afterward, facilitator should have practitioners answer the following questions in a think-pair-share: *What were the risk factors? What were the protective factors? How do you see risk and protective factors operating in your school?* Once done with think-pair-share, the facilitator should allow participants to share the topics discussed. This exercise should take about 20–30 minutes.

2. Facilitator hands out each practitioner Dual-Axis Model of Vulnerability Application Worksheet (see Appendix 15) and divides individuals into grade level, departments, content, or another team configuration. The team configuration should be a group structure in which practitioners typically work with each other on resolving issues. The groups should identify the risk factors found among their group of students and the protective strategies currently operating in their school. This exercise should take about 20–30 minutes. At the end of the exercise, each group should report whether they consider the school is providing sufficient protective strategies to address risk factors.

Colorblindness

As described in Chapter 2, colorblindness as an ideological belief operates with the notion that social identities, specifically race, are constantly muted by individuals outside of a specific racial/ethnic minority group. Additionally, colorblindness rationalizes racial inequality as due to market dynamics, a naturally occurring phenomena (e.g., segregated environments as a self-choice), and racial/ethnic minority groups maintain limiting cultural behaviors (e.g., sagging pants, limited word banks). The following activities are intended to let practitioners think how their colorblindness emerges from limited personalized experiences.

Activity 2.6: My First Racial Memory

Time Required: 1 hour 30 minutes

Materials Required: Racial Timeline Worksheet (see Appendix 16)

Purpose: The goal of the activity is to have practitioners consider the initial memories they have about race and ethnicity, and how those memories affect their current thinking.

Process: The facilitator will provide each practitioner with the Racial Timeline Worksheet. Practitioners can choose to write an event for each or one of the three stages—elementary years, middle and high school years, and college years and beyond. The worksheet should take about 10–15 minutes to complete. After completing the worksheet, practitioners should pair up with someone and begin sharing some of the memories and use the guiding questions on the last page for conversation. This part of the activity should last for 15–20 minutes. The facilitator will then reconvene practitioners as a large group to begin discussing the following questions: *What are some of the personal learnings you gained from the reflections exercise? What are some of the racial memories that your students are developing? How do we help develop healthy racial identities among our students?*

Activity 2.7: Seeing Your Race-Life Journey

Time Required: 1 hour 30 minutes

Materials Required: Racial and Ethnic Group Worksheet (see Appendix 17)

Purpose: The goal of this activity is to let practitioners discuss the racial and ethnic composition of personal friendships they have developed in their life.

Process: The facilitator will begin by finding a large room such as a cafeteria or a gym in which practitioners can move around easily and talk. The facilitator will then label the four corners of the room as "Black and Black Ethnics," "White and White Ethnics," "Latino/a," and "Asian and Pacific Islander" (*Note:* Depending on your community, these labels can be changed to include other specific racial and ethnic groups). The facilitator will guide practitioners to begin in the middle of the room and ask them to think about their elementary-age close friendships and move to the corner of the room that contains the label of the racial and ethnic group that primarily comprised their close friendship circle. Once practitioners are in these corner groups, the facilitator will ask them to discuss with each other the following question: *What are some positive memories you have about these friendships?* Give practitioners about 10–15 minutes to share with each other some of these memories. After the time expires, the facilitator will ask practitioners to consider their middle and high school close friendships and move to the corner with the label of the racial and ethnic group. Again once in their groups, practitioners will answer the same question about positive memories; give them 10–15 minutes. After the time expires, the facilitator will ask practitioners to consider their college/university close friendships and move to the related corner. Again once in their groups, practitioners will answer the same question about positive memories; give them 10–15 minutes. At the end of this last grouping, practitioners should stay standing in their areas and ask the following questions: *What did you notice about your life journey regarding your close friendships? What are some of the themes in the memories shared? Did some of you stay in the same corner for most of your life journey? If so, what does that make you think about your life journey? Did some of you move in or out of various corners? If so, what does that make you think about your life journey?* The facilitator should wrap up this activity by asking practitioners about what it means for them to work with racial/ethnic minority student populations when they do not have enough prior close friendship experiences to assist in providing mental schemas. This exercise elicits practitioners ask questions related to the personal tension—*what can I do*; these conversations should bring up concepts of what it means to engage in equity work at a personal level.

Activity 2.8: Diversity Tables

Note: This activity is adapted from work by Shana Ritter.

Time Required: 50–70 minutes

Materials Required: Large open room space—sufficient size to accommodate staff moving around (activity can be done in an outside playground)

Purpose: Let practitioners explore the various dimensions of social identities that individuals embody.

Process: The facilitator asks practitioners to stand up in the open room space. The facilitator provides the following instructions: A social identity will be shared out to the group, and you are required to find others that consider themselves part of the same social identity as yourself. For example, if the facilitator says "age," practitioners should mill around the room and find others that match their age range. Practitioners are welcome to talk with each other to find the appropriate group. Once in a group, provide practitioners with 8–12 minutes to discuss *what is common about their group* and *what are the misperceptions others have about their group*. Afterward, the activity leader should conduct a round-robin in which each group shares out some of the things discussed in their group. Then the facilitator reads out loud the next social identity and provides the same instructions of time, questions to be discussed, and round-robin sharing. There is only one rule with the activity: once a group is formed, it cannot change.

In closing the activity, the facilitator should reinforce the importance of layered social identities and how these identities are fraught with many experiences that help make sense of the world.

Social Identities

1. Age

2. Favorite sport activity

3. Parents' education

4. Place of birth

5. Ethnicity*

6. Race*

Note: Staff need to gain an understanding that ethnicity is different than race. Ethnicity includes the culture, language, and values of a group. Race is a social construct that assigns categories usually based on physical attributes (i.e., skin color, facial structure, hair). For example, African American is an ethnic identity, and Black is a racial identity.

Activity 2.9a: Replacing Colorblindness Statements

Time Required: 1 hour 30 minutes

Materials Required: Shifting Common Colorblindness Statements Worksheet (see Appendix 18); pens and/or pencils; chart paper and markers

Purpose: The goal of this activity is to have practitioners closely examine colorblindness statements, identify how the statements are problematic, and develop replacement statements.

Process: Each practitioner will receive the Shifting Common Colorblindness Statements Worksheet and get into a small group (two to four individuals). The small group will spend about 15–20 minutes discussing the first two columns of worksheet—the colorblindness phrases and identify color-blindness trait(s). The intention of this first part of the activity is to (1) recognize commonly stated colorblindness-based thoughts, and (2) define how these statements engender a colorblindness trait. Depending on prior knowledge and exposure of the group to the concept, the facilitator may need to walk through several of the statements as a large group and assist facilitators in recognizing statements as colorblind and identifying color-blindness traits. An additional tool that can be shared with the group is the Definition Flashcards (see Appendix 10); this tool can be used as a quick reminder for understanding and identifying colorblindness.

After the small-group exercise, allow two small groups to combine together and discuss their understanding of colorblindness. The intention of this additional small-group debrief is to allow opportunities for practitioners to discuss moving toward a culture consciousness belief system. Such a belief system not only requires practitioners to acknowledge the presence and significance of culture, but also to not apply their own cultural lens as the default or "normal" lens.

Activity 2.9b: Unpacking the Colorblindness Elephant—Survey Activity

Time Required: 1 hour 30 minutes

Materials Required: Shifting Common Colorblindness Statements Survey Worksheet (see Appendix 19)

Purpose: Let practitioners consider how colorblindness as an ideology relies on consistent framing or universalizing culture and minimizing differences of culture and identity.

Process: Each practitioner will receive the Shifting Common Colorblindness Statements Survey Worksheet and respond to each statement with *agree, neutral,* or *disagree.* Give practitioners about 5–8 minutes to complete the survey and remind them that it is anonymous. Afterward, have them fold the survey at least 2 times and place it on a table at the center or front of the room. Once all folded surveys are on the table, move around folded surveys to make sure they are mixed up. Then, ask each practitioner to select a sheet of paper.

The facilitator should identify three sections of the room—agree, neutral, or disagree. Ask each practitioner to open their sheet of paper. The facilitator shall read each statement and allow practitioners to move around the room to the respective corners—agree, neutral, or disagree. Pause in between each statement to allow practitioners to look around and absorb the various perspectives on deficit thoughts. After reading each statement, allow practitioners to pair up and briefly discuss their initial reactions to the various statements. After 5 minutes of paired discussion, the facilitator should lead a large-group conversation using the following questions—*What are some of the topics discussed in your paired group? What statement stood out to you (positive and negative)? What are some other deficit thoughts you hear about racial/ethnic minority or low-income students?*

Activity 2.10: Promoting Cultural Responsibility Beliefs

Time Required: 1 hour 30 minutes

Materials Required: Cultural Responsibility Beliefs Worksheet (see Appendix 20); pens and/or pencils; chart paper and markers

Purpose: The goal of this activity is to have practitioners closely examine cultural responsibility beliefs statements, identify how the statements are affirmative, and develop understanding of personal and professional work necessary to embody these statements.

Process: Each practitioner will receive the Cultural Responsibility Beliefs Worksheet and get into a small group (two to four individuals). The small group will spend about 15–20 minutes discussing the first two columns of worksheet—the cultural responsibility belief statements and identify the cultural affirmation trait(s) in the statement. The intention of this first part of the activity is (1) recognizing commonly stated cultural responsibility thoughts, and (2) defining how these statements engender a cultural affirmation trait. Depending on prior knowledge and exposure of the group to the concept, the facilitator may need to walk through several of the statements as a large group to assist facilitators in recognizing statements as cultural responsibility and identifying the cultural affirmation traits. An additional tool that can be shared with the group is the Definition Flashcards (see Appendix 10); this tool can be used as a quick reminder for understanding and identifying how deficit thinking, poverty disciplining, and colorblindness require replacement beliefs such as cultural responsibility.

After the small-group exercise, allow for two small groups to combine together and discuss their understanding and identification of cultural responsibility. The intention of this additional small-group debrief is to let practitioners discuss with their colleagues these complex concepts and listen to other beliefs.

OTHER ONGOING ACTIVITIES
FOR REPLACING BIASED BELIEFS

Option 1: Video Clip: *Teacher Uses N-Word*

Watch the short clip *Teacher Uses N-Word* (http://www.teachertube .com/video/teacher-uses-n-word-true-story-184675). Respond to the following questions: (1) Is the meaning of the N-word contextual? (2) Who decides what the N-word means? (3) Who (if anyone) has license to use it and when? (4) What does the disagreement about the word suggest about the cultural group that we call "Black" people? (5) Does the use of the N-word have anything to do with one or more of the key concepts we have discussed thus far: culture, identity, power, and privilege? Please explain.

Option 2: Implicit Association Test

Practitioners go online and complete the Implicit Association Test (IAT; https://implicit.harvard.edu/implicit/takeatest.html). Practitioners can bring the results from the test to the next staff development or grade-level meeting and engage in a conversation about the findings. The group should use the following questions: *How do you feel about the results? Are these findings surprising? If so, how? If not, why? Can you think of examples of when these biases show up in your day-to-day interactions.*

Option 3: TED Talks

In the Resources (see Appendix 23), practitioners can select various TED Talks that provide opportunities for considering the impact of color-blindness. One potential TED Talk is the one conducted by Mellody Hobson; she discusses moving away from *colorblindness* to *colorbrave*: www.ted.com/talks/mellody_hobson_color_blind_or_color_brave? language=en. As a follow-up, practitioners can take the definition of color-brave and apply it during professional learning community meetings, grade-level collaborative meetings, staff development, etc.

Another TED Talk is by Chimamanda Ngozi Adichie on the single story that emerges from texts we read and the way it supports narratives among marginalized populations: https://www.ted.com/talks/chimamanda_ adichie_the_danger_of_a_single_story?language=en. As a follow-up, practitioners at each school level can select the list of books students are required to read and examine the narratives of racial/ethnic minority populations.

Option 4: PBS Activities on Race

PBS contains various activities on exploring the complexity of race (www.pbs.org/race). One exercise described is the following: Use the following list of inherited, biological traits to divide people into different groups (sort everyone first using one trait, then resort them using another, and so on, to show how the groups change depending on the criteria): hair color, blood types (A, B, O, A/B), whether or not your tongue curls, lactose tolerance or intolerance (ability to digest milk products), left-handedness or right-handedness, fingerprint types (loop, whorl, arch, or tented arch), skin color (compare the inside of your upper arm), etc.

Follow-Up Questions

- Does the composition of the groups remain consistent from one criterion to the next?
- Is there a clear line of demarcation between groups, or is the boundary more gradual or blurred? Are these criteria any less arbitrary than the physical characteristics we associate with race? Does this exercise mean that race doesn't matter?

This exercise can be used as both an icebreaker and a lesson on how we can be divided into different biological groups depending on the criteria we use. *Note:* This exercise is not meant to demonstrate that we are all the same or that races don't matter. The point is that racial differences are not *biologically based,* but *socially constructed.* This activity can help spark a deeper discussion about the root causes of the disparities raised in the video. Allow 20–30 minutes for the activity and discussion.

Option 5: Name Game

The Name Game is intended to let practitioners consider the social and cultural meaning of names. This activity is an opportunity to assist practitioners understand and develop a culturally conscious perspective, which is a replacement for colorblindness.

Activity instructions: Using a blank sheet of paper, reflect on your name. Feel free to focus on either your full name, middle name, last name, or even a nickname. Each participant should take 5–10 minutes to write his or her reflection. After the reflection, participants should partner with at least two or three other participants and discuss their reflection. This small-group activity should take about 15–20 minutes. After small-group sharing, ask for volunteers to share their reflections, and/or ask for small groups to share some of the conversation topics. As a wrap-up, the participants should be reminded of the importance of names as a symbol of social and cultural fabric that supports moving toward culturally consciousness belief.

Option 6: Understanding Belief Impact on Behavior

The intention of this activity is to let practitioners practice thinking about how beliefs impact practice behavior.

Activity instructions: Each practitioner should partner and choose a belief to discuss from the list provided. Partner 1 will agree with the belief and describe how it might impact behavior. Partner 2 will describe why he or she disagrees with the belief and how that might impact behavior. After defining your "beliefs," discuss your responses to the activity. The partner groups should spend about 15–20 minutes discussing their beliefs. After the partner discussion, a large-group conversation should be conducted to answer the following questions: *Where and when do we see the behaviors appearing in our school setting? How do our kids respond?*

Belief Statements

1. Cultural differences in communication often result in students of color being penalized for the way in which they answer questions.

2. Teachers bring stereotypes that affect their views of students of color, which impact how they teach them.

3. Tougher disciplinary policies will not solve the disciplinary problems of Black or Latino students.

4. I try to ignore skin color to view minority students as individuals.

5. To teach effectively, I need to understand my own culture and values.

6. The things that were done to people of color in the past in this country were terrible, but I am not sure it is the school's responsibility to make up for that.

7. It is rude when Latino students speak Spanish in the classroom.

8. Academically, Asian students do not have to work as hard as other students to get good grades.

9. Black students' cultural attitudes and styles of speech make it hard for me to teach them.

10. Thinking or talking about race makes me feel uncomfortable.

11. Trying to be culturally responsive all the time is nice in theory, but the reality is that a teacher does not have time to be all things to all students.

12. I try to ignore skin color in order to view minority students as individuals.

13. Sometimes I wonder why we can't see each other as individuals instead of race always being an issue.

14. I am sometimes suspicious of data showing racial disparities because data can be manipulated to say anything.

15. I try not to notice a child's race or skin color in the classroom setting.

16. Latino students who speak English should refrain from speaking Spanish at school so they don't to alienate other students or teachers.

APPLICATION ACTIVITIES

As illustrated in the Road Map, the belief awareness activities need to be implemented strategically with application activities. More specifically, practitioners need to have an opportunity to apply new beliefs into everyday school and/or district processes.

Application Activity 1: Affirming Social Identities of Kids—Books

Time Required: 1 hour–1 hour 30 minutes

Materials Required: Sample read-aloud books (elementary); required novels (middle or high school); Looking at Books Worksheet (see Appendix 21)

Purpose: Let practitioners determine whether current book selections affirm racial/ethnic minority students' identities.

Process: Practitioners will convene during staff development with sample books. If it is an elementary school, practitioners shall bring the most recent sample of read-aloud books (K–3) and chapter books/novels (Grades 4–5). If it is a middle or high school, practitioners shall bring the required novels for each grade level. The facilitator should arrange the books around the room in one of two ways; Option 1—if practitioners are arranged in small groups of four to five persons sitting at each table, then a copy of each grade-level book should be placed on every table; and Option 2—facilitator can leave all the books on different of tables or one long table so that practitioners can walk around and examine each book. Depending on the option selected by the facilitator, each practitioner will use the Looking at Books Worksheet to examine each book based on the two columns provided on the worksheet.

Upon completing activity, practitioners should examine the information on their worksheet and discuss with another peer. More specifically, practitioners should discuss the following questions: *Do the books reflect the racial/ethnic, religious, and linguistic diversity of school population? Among the books that reflect racial/ethnic, religious, and linguistic diversity, are the characteristics "heroes or sheroes"? And what are ways to improve the representation and affirmation in our books?* Give practitioners 5–10 minutes to discuss these questions. Afterward, the facilitator should discuss solutions—*what do we do next?* One option the school leader could offer is to use the books from publishers that provide diverse books, for example, Lee and Low Books (www.leeandlow.org), or Scholastic ID (http://teacher.scholastic .com/products/id).

Application Activity 2: Affirming Social Identities of Kids—Classroom Environment

Time Required: 1 hour–1 hour 30 minutes

Materials Required: Observing Classroom Environments Worksheet (see Appendix 22)

Purpose: Let practitioners determine whether their current classrooms affirm racial/ethnic minority and other marginalized students' identities.

Process: Practitioners will convene during staff development with the Observing Classroom Environments Worksheet. The facilitator will instruct the practitioners to go back to their class and use the worksheet to note whether they observe the categories on the worksheet. Practitioners should spend about 10–15 minutes in their classrooms; another option would be to have practitioners go to a peer's classroom and use the worksheet.

Upon completing the activity, practitioners should examine the information on their worksheet and discuss it with another peer. More specifically, practitioners should discuss the following questions: *Do the books reflect the racial/ethnic, religious, and linguistic diversity of school population? Among the books that reflect racial/ethnic, religious, and linguistic diversity, are the characteristics "heroes or sheroes"? And what are ways to improve the representation and affirmation in our books?* Give practitioners about 20 minutes to discuss these questions. Upon completion of paired discussion facilitator should lead a conversation on solutions—*what do we do next?* Options for practitioner is to identify short-term changes they can make to their classrooms. For example, display pictures of students conducting a specific activity, etc. Long-term changes would involve visiting school supply stores to select items that reflect the diversity of society and the student population.

Application Activity 3: Inserting Demographic Criteria in Everyday Practices

This practice aims to encourage practitioners to consider inserting demographic criteria into various practices to rehearse shifting into culture consciousness and identity affirmation beliefs. Table 5.1 provides a range of possible practices.

Table 5.1 Everyday Practices

Practice	Component of Practice	Replacement Practice
Positive Behavioral Intervention Supports	Establishing commitment component	Commitment includes addressing racial/ethnic disparities
	Define schoolwide behavior expectations	Ask various student and adult groups whether expectations are culturally universal
	Teach expectations	Ask various student and adult groups whether expectations are culturally universal
	Process for using data for decision-making	Disaggregate data by race and gender
Professional Learning Community	Data cycle	Disaggregate data by race and gender subgroups and answer why there are performance differences
Restorative Justice	Circle conversation protocol	Ask whether race and/or gender set the stage for the response and action
Instructional Intervention Team or Response-to-Intervention Team	Review of students needing intervention	Examine whether students of similar race and/or gender are being referred by certain practitioners
Literacy Texts and Novels	Purchasing of texts and novels	Examine protagonists and antagonists by race, gender, and religious abilities
Practitioner Hiring Process	Interview process	Pose scenarios in which applicants provide working definition of beliefs that support and detract from student success

Application Activity 4: Adding Culture Consciousness and Identity Affirmation Belief Into Instructional Practice Texts

Practitioners are often conducting book-study sessions throughout the school year. This application activity involves practicing culture consciousness and identity affirmation beliefs alongside these various instructional and behavior-based books. Table 5.2 lists various books for this application activity.

Table 5.2 Sample Books

Book Title and Author	Topic	Culture Consciousness and Identity Affirmation-Driving Question
Choice Words: How Our Language Affects Children's Learning Peter H. Johnston	Language	How does our language use reflect affirming concepts of identity and culture?
Differentiation: From Planning to Practice, Grades 6–12 Rick Wormeli	Instruction	How do differentiation components reflect affirming concepts of identity and culture? Describe the strategies that demonstrate caring relationships based on affirming understanding of culture and identity.
Teach Like a Champion Doug Lemov	Instruction	How do differentiation components reflect affirming concepts of identity and culture? Describe the strategies that demonstrate caring relationships based on affirmative understanding of culture and identity.
Why Are School Buses Yellow? Teaching for Inquiry, K–8 John F. Barell	Instruction	How do inquiry components reflect affirming concepts of identity and culture? Describe the inquiry that is connected to affirmative understanding of culture and identity.
Teach Like Your Hair's on Fire: The Methods and Madness Inside Room 56 Rafe Esquith	Instruction	How do differentiation components reflect affirming concepts of identity and culture? Describe the strategies that demonstrate caring relationships based on affirmative understanding of culture and identity.
Conscious Discipline Becky Bailey	Behavior	How do behavior intervention components reflect affirming concepts of identity and culture? Describe the strategies that demonstrate caring relationships based on affirmative understanding of culture and identity.
Treating Explosive Kids: The Collaborative Problem-Solving Approach Ross W. Greene and J. Stuart Ablon	Behavior	How do behavior intervention components reflect affirming concepts of identity and culture? Describe the strategies that demonstrate caring relationships based on affirmative understanding of culture and identity.
Positive Behavior Facilitation (PBF): Understanding and Intervening in the Behavior of Youth Edna Olive	Behavior	How do behavior intervention components reflect affirming concepts of identity and culture? Describe the strategies that demonstrate caring relationships based on affirmative understanding of culture and identity.

Appendixes

APPENDIX 1: Data Inventory Worksheet

Conduct a data inventory—what do you have, what do you want, who has it, and how can you use it more often?

Purpose: The purpose of a data inventory is to identify information that could potentially be used to understand all the various school conditions.

Process: The data inventory can be distributed to a leadership team as part of meeting in which each person contributes from his or her vantage the set of data they interface.

Data Inventory

Grade Levels: _____

Use this to keep track of the available data for your equity work.

Data Type (e.g., test, survey, observation)	What Does It Measure or Examine	Quantitative or Qualitative	Data Name	Who Collects the Data	When Is It Collected	Subject (e.g., student, teacher, parent, building)

In completing this inventory, keep the following in mind:

- What data do we still need? Can we collect these data with the tools we have? Do we need to create a new tool?
- Is there a balance of qualitative and quantitative data?
- Do we have data on multiple levels (individual, class, school, district, community)?

Copyright © 2017 by Corwin. All rights reserved. Reprinted from *Solving Disproportionality and Achieving Equity: A Leader's Guide to Using Data to Change Hearts and Minds* by Edward Fergus. Thousand Oaks, CA: Corwin, www.corwin.com. Reproduction authorized only for the local school site or nonprofit organization that has purchased this book.

APPENDIX 2: Planning Sheet for Addressing Beliefs and Building Equity Principles

Goal: 1. Create equity principles for school year.

2. Create new affirmative beliefs to support equity principles.

	August–October	November–January	February–April	May–June
Building Equity Principles Activities				
Addressing Bias-Based Beliefs Activities				

Copyright © 2017 by Corwin. All rights reserved. Reprinted from *Solving Disproportionality and Achieving Equity: A Leader's Guide to Using Data to Change Hearts and Minds* by Edward Fergus. Thousand Oaks, CA: Corwin, www.corwin.com. Reproduction authorized only for the local school site or nonprofit organization that has purchased this book.

Exit Ticket

Please check the appropriate box.

Workshop Content and Activities	Very Helpful	Somewhat Helpful	Not Helpful at All	Did Not Attend
I found the content of the training . . .	☐	☐	☐	☐
I found the activities of the training . . .	☐	☐	☐	☐
I found the resources of the training . . .	☐	☐	☐	☐
I found the structure of the training . . .	☐	☐	☐	☐

Please list any new learning that you acquired as a result of the training.

1. _____
2. _____
3. _____

Please list any additional information you would like to receive as a result of this training.

_____
_____
_____

✂--

Exit Ticket

Please check the appropriate box.

Workshop Content and Activities	Very Helpful	Somewhat Helpful	Not Helpful at All	Did Not Attend
I found the content of the training . . .	☐	☐	☐	☐
I found the activities of the training . . .	☐	☐	☐	☐
I found the resources of the training . . .	☐	☐	☐	☐
I found the structure of the training . . .	☐	☐	☐	☐

Please list any new learning that you acquired as a result of the training.

1. _____
2. _____
3. _____

Please list any additional information you would like to receive as a result of this training.

_____
_____
_____

Copyright © 2017 by Corwin. All rights reserved. Reprinted from *Solving Disproportionality and Achieving Equity: A Leader's Guide to Using Data to Change Hearts and Minds* by Edward Fergus. Thousand Oaks, CA: Corwin, www.corwin.com. Reproduction authorized only for the local school site or nonprofit organization that has purchased this book.

APPENDIX 4: Definitions of Educational Equity Worksheet

Definitions of Educational Equity

Enid Lee (2002)

"The principle of altering current practices and perspectives to teach for social transformation and to promote equitable learning outcomes for students for all social groups."

Glenn Singleton (2015)

"Equity in education is raising the achievement of all students while: narrowing the gaps between the highest- and lowest-performing students; and eliminating the racial predictability and disproportionality of which student groups occupy the highest and lowest achievement categories."

Edward Fergus (2016)

"Equity is seeing someone differently in order to treat them fairly. The idea is each individual has unique dynamics of how they have experienced society and such experiences must be taken into consideration in defining the equitable practice necessary to achieve the desired outcome. For example, if I'm teaching the history of agriculture in the US to students from a rural farming community without taking in their experiences would mean not harnessing their knowledge base."

H. Richard Milner (2010)

"People's beliefs about race informed by the areas outlined above shape what they do and do not do in practice. Although race is a central construct used to examine educational outcomes, policies, and practices, the depth and breadth of its applications are limited in public and academic discourse. For instance, people often talk about an 'achievement gap' and disparities between white and black/brown students. However, race is not treated in any substantive way beyond reporting the data outcomes."

Gloria Ladson-Billings (1994)

"I have defined culturally relevant teaching as a pedagogy of opposition (1992c) not unlike critical pedagogy but specifically committed to collective, not merely individual, empowerment. Culturally relevant pedagogy rests on three criteria or propositions: (a) Students must experience academic success; (b) students must develop and/or maintain cultural competence; and (c) students must develop a critical consciousness through which they challenge the status quo of the current social order."

(Continued)

(Continued)

Responding to Definitions of Educational Equity

	What Resonates	What Is Unclear	What Do You Absorb
Enid Lee			
Glenn Singleton			
Edward Fergus			
H. Richard Milner			
Gloria Ladson-Billings			

Copyright © 2017 by Corwin. All rights reserved. Reprinted from *Solving Disproportionality and Achieving Equity: A Leader's Guide to Using Data to Change Hearts and Minds* by Edward Fergus. Thousand Oaks, CA: Corwin, www.corwin.com. Reproduction authorized only for the local school site or nonprofit organization that has purchased this book.

APPENDIX 5: Applying Definitions of Educational Equity

Instructions: Download one of the following pictures to use in answering the following questions:

- http://interactioninstitute.org/wp-content/uploads/2016/01/IISC_EqualityEquity.png
- http://9gag.com/gag/ajAerM1/equality-vs-equity

How does this picture demonstrate equity?	
What is challenging about both pictures?	
Which picture reflects your current state of equity?	

Copyright © 2017 by Corwin. All rights reserved. Reprinted from *Solving Disproportionality and Achieving Equity: A Leader's Guide to Using Data to Change Hearts and Minds* by Edward Fergus. Thousand Oaks, CA: Corwin, www.corwin.com. Reproduction authorized only for the local school site or nonprofit organization that has purchased this book.

	Practice 1: _____	Practice 2: _____
Enid Lee		
Glenn Singleton		
Edward Fergus		
H. Richard Milner		
Gloria Ladson-Billings		

Copyright © 2017 by Corwin. All rights reserved. Reprinted from *Solving Disproportionality and Achieving Equity: A Leader's Guide to Using Data to Change Hearts and Minds* by Edward Fergus. Thousand Oaks, CA: Corwin, www.corwin.com. Reproduction authorized only for the local school site or nonprofit organization that has purchased this book.

Individual	Pair

Quad	Octet

Copyright © 2017 by Corwin. All rights reserved. Reprinted from *Solving Disproportionality and Achieving Equity: A Leader's Guide to Using Data to Change Hearts and Minds* by Edward Fergus. Thousand Oaks, CA: Corwin, www.corwin.com. Reproduction authorized only for the local school site or nonprofit organization that has purchased this book.

Sample Deficit-Thinking Phrases

Deficit-Based Thoughts	Identify Deficit Trait(s)	Unlearn Deficit-Based Thoughts: Consider re-defining the problem as not solely the population, but also the structural inequalities.
Students of color from disadvantaged homes just seem to show a lack of initiative.		E.g., students of color from disadvantaged homes are disproportionately being suspended and receive limited access to enrichment, and thus are challenged to show initiative.
Disadvantaged students generally do not have the abilities necessary to succeed in the classroom.		
Students from disadvantaged backgrounds do not value education as much as other students.		
It is important that students of color assimilate so that they can succeed in mainstream American culture.		E.g., it is important that schools understand and embrace the cultural assets of students of color so that they can learn how to have cross-cultural experiences in schools and society.
Unfortunately, for many people of color, education is just not a real priority.		
Schools cannot be expected to overcome the disadvantages of race and poverty.		

(Continued)

(Continued)

There is not much schools can do to close the achievement gap.		
Trying to be culturally responsive all the time is nice in theory, but the reality is that a teacher does not have time to be all things to all students.		
I am frustrated by how hard it is to be politically correct in our more diverse society.		
The values and beliefs shared by those in disadvantaged neighborhoods tend to go against school values and beliefs about what makes up a good education.		E.g., continuous social experiences of discrimination and structural disadvantage make it hard to believe that merit will result in success.
As an educator, I'm very limited in what I can do when students from disadvantaged neighborhoods hold negative beliefs about their education.		
Racial/ethnic minority children from disadvantaged neighborhoods do not have the role models they need to be successful in school.		
Although I am hesitant to say so publicly, I believe that racial differences in intelligence may have a hereditary or genetic component.		

Copyright © 2017 by Corwin. All rights reserved. Reprinted from *Solving Disproportionality and Achieving Equity: A Leader's Guide to Using Data to Change Hearts and Minds* by Edward Fergus. Thousand Oaks, CA: Corwin, www.corwin.com. Reproduction authorized only for the local school site or nonprofit organization that has purchased this book.

Sample Deficit-Thinking Phrases

Deficit-Based Thoughts	Agree	Neutral	Disagree
Students of color from disadvantaged homes just seem to show a lack of initiative.			
Disadvantaged students generally do not have the abilities necessary to succeed in the classroom.			
Students from disadvantaged backgrounds do not value education as much as other students.			
It is important that students of color assimilate so that they can succeed in mainstream American culture.			
Unfortunately, for many people of color, education is just not a real priority.			
Schools cannot be expected to overcome the disadvantages of race and poverty.			
There is not much schools can do to close the achievement gap.			
Trying to be culturally responsive all the time is nice in theory, but the reality is that a teacher does not have time to be all things to all students.			
I am frustrated by how hard it is to be politically correct in our more diverse society.			
The values and beliefs shared by those in disadvantaged neighborhoods tend to go against school values and beliefs about what makes up a good education.			
As an educator, I'm very limited in what I can do when students from disadvantaged neighborhoods hold negative beliefs about their education.			
African American children from disadvantaged neighborhoods do not have the role models they need to be successful in school.			
Although I am hesitant to say so publicly, I believe that racial differences in intelligence may have a hereditary or genetic component.			

Copyright © 2017 by Corwin. All rights reserved. Reprinted from *Solving Disproportionality and Achieving Equity: A Leader's Guide to Using Data to Change Hearts and Minds* by Edward Fergus. Thousand Oaks, CA: Corwin, www.corwin.com. Reproduction authorized only for the local school site or nonprofit organization that has purchased this book.

Deficit Thinking **Definition:** An ideology used to explain academic performance and at times cognitive abilities as result of deficiencies within a cultural group. It additionally minimizes the influence of systemic patterns on abilities and behaviors.	**Deficit Thinking** **Checklist Traits:** • Blames cultural group for ability or behavior • Does not acknowledge systemic problems • Creates and/or supports a stereotype of a cultural group
Colorblindness **Definition:** A belief that promotes the idea that the best way to remove racism is to omit race, gender, and other social identities as a descriptor. Instead, it involves treating individuals as individuals and not considering their social identities and focuses on discussing and framing the commonalities between individuals. The default identity in this ideology is Whiteness.	**Colorblindness** **Checklist Traits:** • Omits social identities that differ from White, male, and/or heterosexual • Insists on utilization of commonalities versus differences language
Poverty Disciplining **Definition:** A belief that considers changing the behavioral and psychological dispositions of low-income individuals as paramount to fixing their low-income condition. In other words, deficit-thinking bias is focused on a set of beliefs about ability, while poverty disciplining bias is focused on changing behavior and thinking of low-income individuals.	**Poverty Disciplining** **Checklist Traits:** • Insists on changing behavior and psychological dispositions • Disciplining promotes "good citizenship" behaviors

Copyright © 2017 by Corwin. All rights reserved. Reprinted from *Solving Disproportionality and Achieving Equity: A Leader's Guide to Using Data to Change Hearts and Minds* by Edward Fergus. Thousand Oaks, CA: Corwin, www.corwin.com. Reproduction authorized only for the local school site or nonprofit organization that has purchased this book.

APPENDIX 11: Shifting Poverty-Disciplining Belief Statements Worksheet

	Translations or What Is Often Meant	Replacement Narrative
Disciplinary action should be taken against students who wear sagging clothes in school.		
Latino students who speak English should refrain from speaking Spanish at school so they assimilate into American society.		
Poor families are able to achieve success if they learn how to speak more articulately.		
Low-income students who qualify for special education are probably in home environments with limited reading and language.		
Behaviors like respect and self-regulation are traits that low-income students require learning more often than not.		
A good way to teach low-income students to be successful in school is to provide them classes on proper character and behaviors.		
Parent involvement workshops for low-income families should focus on helping them learn the most important elements of school.		
The values and beliefs shared by those in disadvantaged neighborhoods tend to go against school values and beliefs about what makes up a good education.		

Copyright © 2017 by Corwin. All rights reserved. Reprinted from *Solving Disproportionality and Achieving Equity: A Leader's Guide to Using Data to Change Hearts and Minds* by Edward Fergus. Thousand Oaks, CA: Corwin, www.corwin.com. Reproduction authorized only for the local school site or nonprofit organization that has purchased this book.

APPENDIX 12: Shifting Poverty-Disciplining Belief Statements Survey Worksheet

	Agree	Neutral	Disagree
Disciplinary action should be taken against students who wear sagging clothes in school.			
Latino students who speak English should refrain from speaking Spanish at school so they assimilate into American society.			
Poor families are able to achieve success if they learn how to speak more articulately.			
Low-income students who qualify for special education are probably in home environments with limited reading and language.			
Behaviors like respect and self-regulation are traits that low-income students require learning more often than not.			
A good way to teach low-income students to be successful in school is to provide them classes on proper character and behaviors.			
Parent involvement workshops for low-income families should focus on helping them learn the most important elements of school.			
The values and beliefs shared by those in disadvantaged neighborhoods tend to go against school values and beliefs about what makes up a good education.			

Copyright © 2017 by Corwin. All rights reserved. Reprinted from *Solving Disproportionality and Achieving Equity: A Leader's Guide to Using Data to Change Hearts and Minds* by Edward Fergus. Thousand Oaks, CA: Corwin, www.corwin.com. Reproduction authorized only for the local school site or nonprofit organization that has purchased this book.

Everyone starts out standing on a line in the middle of the room facing one wall. Participants are told that the line is the starting line for how they began their life. Participants are asked to silently take a step forward or back, depending on given instructions and if a statement of social status applies to them or not. They may decide for themselves whether the statement applies and, as much as possible, keep their steps the same size throughout the exercise. Explain that the exercise will be done in silence to allow participants to notice the feelings that come up during the exercise and to make it safer for all participants. Also explain that it is their choice to respond to each statement.

This part of the activity will take about 15–20 minutes.

Stage 1

Use the following statements.

1. If you feel that your primary ethnic identity is "American," take one step forward.

2. If you were ever called names or ridiculed because of your race, ethnicity, or class background or gender identity, take one step backward.

3. If you grew up with racial/ethnic minority or working-class people who were servants, maids, gardeners, or babysitters in your house, take one step forward.

4. If you were ever embarrassed or ashamed of your clothes, your house, or your family car when growing up, take one step backward.

5. If you have immediate family members who are doctors, lawyers, or other professionals, take one step forward.

6. If illegal activities were a major occupational alternative in the community where you were raised, take one step backward.

7. If you ever tried to change your physical appearance, mannerisms, language, or behavior to avoid being judged or ridiculed, take one step backward.

8. If you studied the history and culture of your ethnic ancestors in elementary and secondary school, take one step forward.

9. If you started school speaking a language other than English, take one step backward.

10. If your parents or grandparents were able to buy or rent a home in any neighborhood, take one step forward.

11. If you ever skipped a meal or went away from a meal hungry because there wasn't enough money to buy food in your family, take one step backward.

(Continued)

(Continued)

12. If you were taken to art galleries, museums, or plays by your parents, take one step forward.

13. If one of your parents was ever laid off, unemployed, or underemployed, take one step backward.

14. If you ever attended a private school or summer camp, take one step forward.

15. If you received less encouragement in academics or sports from your family or from teachers because of your gender, take one step backward.

16. If you or your family ever had to move because there wasn't enough money to pay the rent, take one step backward.

17. If you were told by your parents that you were beautiful, smart, and capable of achieving your dreams, take two steps forward.

18. If you were told by your parents that you were beautiful, pretty, or good looking and therefore what you thought or did wasn't important, take one step backward.

19. If you can go shopping most of the time pretty sure that you will not be followed or harassed, take one step forward.

20. If you have to deal with catcalls because of your gender, take one step backward.

Stage 2

Once statements are complete, allow participants to ponder their movement.

1. Look to your left, right, forward, and back. Consider how you got to this point.

2. Turn to your neighbors nearest to you and create a small group of three to five individuals. Discuss with each other the following questions: What statements stood out for you, what memories of your journey did these statements remind you, and how do you think your students would do if responding to some of these statements?

Copyright © 2017 by Corwin. All rights reserved. Reprinted from *Solving Disproportionality and Achieving Equity: A Leader's Guide to Using Data to Change Hearts and Minds* by Edward Fergus. Thousand Oaks, CA: Corwin, www.corwin.com. Reproduction authorized only for the local school site or nonprofit organization that has purchased this book.

Risk Factor Level		
	High	**Low**
Protective Factor Level — Low	High Vulnerability (difficulties apparent)	Masked Vulnerability (difficulties veiled)
Protective Factor Level — High	Low Vulnerability (demonstrated, but often unacknowledged resilience)	Undetermined Vulnerability (positive outcomes predicted)

Source: Adapted from Spencer (2006)

Risk Factors	Protective Strategies

Copyright © 2017 by Corwin. All rights reserved. Reprinted from *Solving Disproportionality and Achieving Equity: A Leader's Guide to Using Data to Change Hearts and Minds* by Edward Fergus. Thousand Oaks, CA: Corwin, www.corwin.com. Reproduction authorized only for the local school site or nonprofit organization that has purchased this book.

APPENDIX 16: Racial Timeline Worksheet

Directions: In the following pages, you will create a timeline of racial experiences that contributed to shaping your awareness of race in America. You will be asked to think of several events/experiences during different stages in your life that contributed to your understanding of what it means to be of a particular race, as well as how you learned to perceive others who do not share your racial background. In order to accomplish this task, please do the following:

1. Briefly describe the event and be sure to include (if possible) the approximate age when you experienced it.

2. Explain the message around race you internalized or heard from your experience.

3. Answer the questions at the end of this exercise.

The purpose of this exercise is to highlight both subtle and direct environmental messages that have influenced your development of many of the internal biases you may have about yourself and others. As you do this activity, you may find that you have experienced many different messages at different points in your life, perhaps even leading you to develop multiple ideas around race, which is normal. *What is important to remember is to be open and forthcoming and know that there are no right or wrong answers. This is an exercise in personal reflection; therefore, all who participate must avoid engaging in character judgment!*

(Continued)

(Continued)

Elementary Years and Earlier

Event_____

_____

_____

_____

Message_____

_____

_____

_____

Middle and High School Years

Event_____

_____

_____

_____

Message_____

_____

_____

_____

College Years and Beyond

Event_____

_____

_____

_____

Message_____

_____

_____

_____

(Continued)

(Continued)

Please respond to the following questions in group-sharing component.

1. What events shaped my awareness (or lack of awareness) of my race?

2. When did I first realize that I am _____?

3. What events shaped my perceptions of other racial groups?

4. In what ways do I inadvertently act out on these biases in the classroom or with the students and families I work with?

5. What actions will I take to avoid acting on these biases? How will I hold others accountable?

Copyright © 2017 by Corwin. All rights reserved. Reprinted from *Solving Disproportionality and Achieving Equity: A Leader's Guide to Using Data to Change Hearts and Minds* by Edward Fergus. Thousand Oaks, CA: Corwin, www.corwin.com. Reproduction authorized only for the local school site or nonprofit organization that has purchased this book.

BLACK AND BLACK ETHNICS

WHITE AND WHITE ETHNICS

LATINO/ HISPANIC

NATIVE AMERICANS OR FIRST PEOPLES

ASIAN

PACIFIC ISLANDERS

APPENDIX 18: Shifting Common Colorblindness Statements Worksheet

	Translations or What Is Often Meant	Replacement Narrative
I try to ignore skin color in order to view minority students as individuals.		
Sometimes I wonder why we can't see each other as individuals instead of race always being an issue.		
The things that were done to people of color in the past in this country were terrible, but I am not sure it is the school's responsibility to make up for that.		
Disciplinary action should be taken against students who wear sagging clothes in school.		
I am sometimes suspicious of data showing racial disparities because data can be manipulated to say anything.		
It is rude when Latino students speak Spanish in the classroom.		
I try not to notice a child's race or skin color in the classroom setting.		
Latino students who speak English should refrain from speaking Spanish at school so they don't to alienate other students or teachers.		
Regardless of family background, schools and classrooms cannot afford to make exceptions to disciplinary policy.		
Racism would cease to exist if everyone would just forget about race and see each other as human beings.		

Copyright © 2017 by Corwin. All rights reserved. Reprinted from *Solving Disproportionality and Achieving Equity: A Leader's Guide to Using Data to Change Hearts and Minds* by Edward Fergus. Thousand Oaks, CA: Corwin, www.corwin.com. Reproduction authorized only for the local school site or nonprofit organization that has purchased this book.

	Agree	Neutral	Disagree
I try to ignore skin color in order to view minority students as individuals.			
Sometimes I wonder why we can't see each other as individuals instead of race always being an issue.			
The things that were done to people of color in the past in this country were terrible, but I am not sure it is the school's responsibility to make up for that.			
Disciplinary action should be taken against students who wear sagging clothes in school.			
I am sometimes suspicious of data showing racial disparities because data can be manipulated to say anything.			
It is rude when Latino students speak Spanish in the classroom.			
I try not to notice a child's race or skin color in the classroom setting.			
Latino students who speak English should refrain from speaking Spanish at school so they don't to alienate other students or teachers.			
Regardless of family background, schools and classrooms cannot afford to make exceptions to disciplinary policy.			
Racism would cease to exist if everyone would just forget about race and see each other as human beings.			

Copyright © 2017 by Corwin. All rights reserved. Reprinted from *Solving Disproportionality and Achieving Equity: A Leader's Guide to Using Data to Change Hearts and Minds* by Edward Fergus. Thousand Oaks, CA: Corwin, www.corwin.com. Reproduction authorized only for the local school site or nonprofit organization that has purchased this book.

APPENDIX 20: Cultural Responsibility Beliefs Worksheet

	What does belief statement affirm?	What are the personal and professional challenges of practicing such a belief?
As an educator, it is my responsibility to learn about a child's race and/or culture and how it affects his or her performance in the classroom.		
Each race has its own distinctive characteristics.		
It is up to me as an educator to make sure that all children succeed regardless of the cultural values.		
It is up to me as an educator to make sure that all children succeed regardless of the disadvantages they bring with them.		
As a teacher, it is my responsibility to raise questions about the ways the school system serves students of color.		
In order to teach effectively, I need to understand my own culture and values.		
A teacher has the responsibility to stay current with new and effective ways to incorporate culture into the classroom.		
Schools have a responsibility to provide services to students of color that will help them overcome the disadvantages they have faced.		
I make changes to my instruction to accommodate my students' culture on a daily basis.		
Ethnicity is part of who students are.		
It is my responsibility to learn about cultural differences between students of color.		
I have a responsibility to adapt instruction to account for cultural differences among my students.		

Copyright © 2017 by Corwin. All rights reserved. Reprinted from *Solving Disproportionality and Achieving Equity: A Leader's Guide to Using Data to Change Hearts and Minds* by Edward Fergus. Thousand Oaks, CA: Corwin, www.corwin.com. Reproduction authorized only for the local school site or nonprofit organization that has purchased this book.

Name of Book	Humans or Animals as Main Characters (Yes or No)	Racial/Ethnic, Linguistic, and/or Religious Identity of Protagonist (P) and Antagonist (A)

Copyright © 2017 by Corwin. All rights reserved. Reprinted from *Solving Disproportionality and Achieving Equity: A Leader's Guide to Using Data to Change Hearts and Minds* by Edward Fergus. Thousand Oaks, CA: Corwin, www.corwin.com. Reproduction authorized only for the local school site or nonprofit organization that has purchased this book.

APPENDIX 22: Observing Classroom Environments Worksheet

	Observed	Not Observed	Not Applicable
Bulletin boards, displays, instructional materials, and other visuals in the classroom reflect the racial, ethnic, and cultural backgrounds of students.			
Use of visual aids and props include multiethnic representations			
At least half of the books in the classroom library contains books with covers that demonstrate multiple ethnic groups, gender, and physical abilities.			
Displays with some words in students' heritage language.			
Student work products are displayed in the classroom.			
Students are greeted when entering the classroom.			
Additional Observations (include below)			

Copyright © 2017 by Corwin. All rights reserved. Reprinted from *Solving Disproportionality and Achieving Equity: A Leader's Guide to Using Data to Change Hearts and Minds* by Edward Fergus. Thousand Oaks, CA: Corwin, www.corwin.com. Reproduction authorized only for the local school site or nonprofit organization that has purchased this book.

Resources on Colorblindness

Articles and Books

Bonilla-Silva, E. (2006). Racism with racists: Color-blind racism and persistence of racial inequality in the United States. New York, NY: Rowman & Littlefield.

Cross, W. E., Jr. (1991). *Shades of Black: Diversity in African American identity.* Philadelphia PA: Temple University Press.

Phinney, J. S. (1990). Ethnic identity in adolescents and adults: A review of research. *Psychological Bulletin, 108,* 499–514.

Tatum, B. (1992, April). Talking about race, learning about racism: The application of racial identity development theory in the classroom. *Harvard Educational Review, 62*(1), 1–25.

Tatum, B. D. (2003). "Why are all the black kids sitting together in the cafeteria?": A psychologist explains the development of racial identity (5th anniv., rev. ed.). New York, NY: Basic Books.

Tatum, B. D. (2007). *Can we talk about race? and other conversations in an era of school resegregation.* Boston, MA: Beacon Press.

Teel, K. M., & Obidah, J. E. (2008). *Building racial and cultural competence in the classroom.* New York, NY: Teachers College.

Websites

Mellody Hobson TED Talk on moving away from colorblindness to colorbrave. Retrieved from https://www.ted.com/talks/mellody_hobson_color_blind_or_color_brave?language=en

Racial Inventory questionnaire. Retrieved from http://www.whatsrace.org/images/inventory.pdf

What's Race Got to Do with It? Series. http://www.whatsrace.org

Resources on Deficit Thinking

Articles and Books

Gorski, P. (2010). Unlearning deficit thinking and the scornful gaze. Retrieved from http://www.edchange.org/publications/deficit-ideology-scornful-gaze.pdf

Valencia, R. (2010). *Dismantling contemporary deficit thinking: Educational thought and practice.* New York, NY: Taylor & Francis.

Weiner, L. (2006, September). Challenging deficit thinking. *Educational Leadership, 64*(1).

Websites

Rita Pierson, educator discusses the importance of seeing the potential of children. Retrieved from https://www.ted.com/speakers/rita_f_pierson

Project Implicit is an online resource for testing hidden biases. Retrieved from https://implicit.harvard.edu/implicit/

Resources on Culturally Responsive Education

Ahuha, G. (2009, March 23). What a doll tells us about race. [Video file]. Retrieved from http://abcnews.go.com/GMA/story?id=7213714&page=1

Algozzine, B., O'Shea, D. J., & Obiakor, F. E. (2009). *Culturally responsive literacy instruction.* Thousand Oaks, CA: Corwin.

Bronson, P., & Merryman, A. (2009, September 14). See baby discriminate. [Audio file]. Retrieved from http://www.newsweek.com/id214989

Conchas, G. Q. (2006) *The color of success.* New York, NY: Teachers College.

Cushman, K. (1999). The cycle of inquiry and action: Essential learning communities. *Horace,15*(4). Retrieved May 2007 from http://www.essentialschools.org/cs/resources/view/ces-res/74

Decker, D. M., Dona, D. P., & Christenson, S. L. (2007). Behaviorally at-risk African American students: The importance of student-teacher relationships for student outcomes. *Journal of School Psychology, 45*(1), 83–109. EJ748944: http://www.eric.ed.gov/ERICWebPortabl/custom/portlets/recordDetails/detailmini.jsp_nfpb=ture&_&EROCExtSearch_Search_SearchValue_0=EJ748944&ERICxtSearch_SearchType_0-no&acCno=EJ748944

Delpit, L. (1993). Other people's children: Cultural conflict in the classroom. New York, NY: The New Press.

Fashola, O. S. (2005). *Educating African American males voices from the field.* Thousand Oaks, CA: Corwin.

Fergus, E. (2004). *Skin Color and identity formation: Perceptions of opportunity and academic orientation among Mexican and Puerto Rican youth.* New York, NY: Routledge.

Ferguson, R. F. (2008). *Toward excellence with equity an emerging vision for closing the achievement gap.* Cambridge, MA: Harvard Education Press.

Gay, G. (2002). Preparing for culturally responsive teaching. *Journal of Teacher Education, 53*(2), 106.

Gay, G. (2000). *Culturally responsive teaching: Theory, research, and practice.* New York, NY: Teachers College Press.

Gorski, P. (2008). The myth of the "culture of poverty." *Educational Leadership, 65*(7), 32–37.

Haager, D., & Klingner, J. K. (2004). Strategies for differentiating instruction. In E. R. Hollins, *Culture in school learning.* New Jersey, NJ: Lawrence Erlbaum Associates.

Irvine, J. J., & Armento, B. J. (2001). *Culturally responsive teaching: Lesson planning for elementary and middle grades.* New York, NY: The McGraw Hill.

Jackson, Y. (2011). *The pedagogy of confidence: Inspiring high intellectual performance in urban schools.* New York, NY: Teachers College Press.

Kozleski, E. B., Sobel, D., & Taylor, S. (2003). Addressing issues of disproportionality: Embracing and building culturally responsive practices. *Multiple Voices for Ethnically Diverse Exceptional Learners, 6,* 73–87.

Ladson-Billings, G. (1994). *The dreamkeepers: Successful teachers of African American children.* San Fransisco, CA: Jossey-Bass.

McLaughlin, M., & Mitra, D. (2004). *The cycle of inquiry as the engine of school reform: Lessons from the Bay Area School Reform Collaborative.* Stanford, CA: Center for Research on the Context of Teaching.

Milner, H. R. (2013). *Start where you are, but don't stay there.* Cambridge, MA: Harvard Education Press.

Mithaug, D. E. (1996). *Equal opportunity theory.* Thousand Oaks, CA: Sage.

Moats, L. C. (1999). Teaching reading is rocket science: What expert teachers of reading should know and be able to do. Washington, DC: American Federation of Teachers.

National Association of School Psychologists. (2003). *Portraits of children: Culturally competent assessment.* Bethesda, MD: Author.

National Center for Culturally Responsive Educational Systems. See tools for states and districts to use as they work to implement a quality, culturally responsive education for all students at http://www.nccrest.org/publica tions/tools.html

National Dissemination Center for Children with Disabilities (NICHCY). (2007). *Building the legacy: A training curriculum on IDEA, disproportionality and overrepresentation module.* Retrieved May 2007, from http://www.nichcy. org/training/contents.asp

Nieto, S. (1999). *The light in their eyes: creating multicultural learning communities.* New York, NY: Teachers College Press.

Noguera, P., Hurtado, A., & Fergus, E. (Eds.). (2011). *Invisible no more: Understanding the disenfranchisement of Latino boys and men.* New York, NY: Routledge.

Noguera, P. A. (2008). *The trouble with Black boys . . . And other reflections on race, equity, and the future of public education.* San Fransisco, CA: Jossey-Bass.

Purdie-Vaughns, V., Cohen, G. L., Garcia, J., Sumner, R., Cook, J. C., & Apfel, N. (2009, September 23). Improving minority academic performance: How a values-affirmation intervention works. *Teachers College Record.* Retrieved from http://www.tcrecord.org.

Rodriguez, E. R., & Bellanca, J. (2007). *What is it about me you can't teach?* (2nd ed.). Thousand Oaks, CA: Corwin.

Salend, S. J. (2005). *Creating inclusive classrooms: Effective and reflective practices* (5th ed.) Columbus, OH: Merrill/Prentice Hall.

Tatum, B. D. (2003). "Why are all the black kids sitting together in the cafeteria?": A psychologist explains the development of racial identity (5th anniv., rev. ed.). New York, NY: Basic Books.

Tatum, B. D. (2007). Can we talk about race? and other conversations in an era of school resegregation. Boston, MA: Beacon Press.

Teel, K. M., & Obidah, J. E. (2008). *Building racial and cultural competence in the classroom.* New York, NY: Teachers College.

Resources on Disproportionality in Special Education

Ahram, R., & Fergus, E. (2011). Understanding disproportionality: Views in suburban schools. In A. Artiles, E. Kozleski, & F. Waitoller, (Eds.), *Equity in inclusive education in four continents: A cultural historical multilevel model.* Cambridge, MA: Harvard Education Press.

Ahram, R., Stembridge, A., Fergus, E., & Noguera, P. (2011). *Framing urban school challenges: Problems to examine before implementing response to intervention.* New York, NY: National Center for Learning Disabilities.

Artiles, A. J., & Harry, B. (2004). Addressing culturally and linguistically diverse student overrepresentation in special education: guidelines for parents. The National Center for Culturally and Linguistically Educational Systems (NCCRESt). Retrieved from http://www.nccrest.org

Artiles, A. J., & Rueda, R. (2002, March–April). General guidelines for monitoring minority overrepresentation in special education. *CASE Newsletter, 43*(5), 5–6.

Avoké, S. K., & Wood-Garnett, S. (2001). Language minority children and youth in special education. *Teaching Exceptional Children, 33*(4), 90–91.

Burnette, J. (1998). *Reducing the disproportionate representation of minority students in special education (ED417501).* ERIC/OSEP Digest #E566. Reston, VA: ERIC Clearinghouse on Disabilities and Gifted Education.

Daniels, V. I. (1998). Minority students in gifted and special education programs: The case for educational equity. *Journal of Special Education, 32,* 41–43.

Donovan, M. S., & Cross, C. T. (Eds.). (2002). *Minority students in special and gifted education.* Washington, DC: National Academy Press.

Fergus, E. (2010). *Common causes of disproportionality. California Department of Education Special Education Newsletter, 23*(3), 1–8.

Fergus, E. (2010). Distinguishing cultural difference from disability: Common causes of disproportionality. Equity Alliance at Arizona State University.

Fergus, E. (2010). Common causes of disproportionality. Leadscape Blog. Retrieved from http://www.niusileadscape.org/bl/?p=433

Ford, D. Y. (1998). The under-representation of minority students in gifted education: Problems and promises in recruitment and retention. *Journal of Special Education, 32,* 4–14.

Foster, S. (2001, March 2). Harvard studies find inappropriate special education placements continue to segregate and limit educational opportunities for minority students nationwide. *HGSE News.* Retrieved from http://www.gse.harvard.edu/news/features/speced03022001.html

Harry, B., & Klingner, J. (2006). *Why are so many minority students in special education? Understanding race and disability in schools.* New York, NY: Teachers College Press.

Ladner, M., & Hammons, C. (2001). Special but unequal: Race and special education. In C. E. Fenn, Jr., A. J. Rotherham, & C. R. Hokanson (Eds.), *Rethinking special education for a new century* (pp. 85–110). Washington, DC: Thomas B. Fordham Foundation.

MacMillan, D. L., & Reschly, D. J. (1998). Overrepresentation of minority students: The case for greater specificity or reconsideration of the variables examined. *Journal of Special Education, 32,* 15–24.

Markowitz, J., Garcia, S. B., & Eichelberger, J. H. (1997). Addressing the disproportionate representation of students from racial and ethnic minority groups in special education: A resource document (ED 406 810 – Microfiche, 115 pages). Alexandria, VA: National Association of State Directors of Special Education.

Morales-James, C., Lopez, L., Wilkins, R., & Fergus, E. (2011). *Cultural adaptations to implementation of RTI.* National Center for Learning Disabilities.

Naglieri, J. A., & Rojahn, J. (2001). Intellectual classification of black and white children in special education programs using the WISC-III and the Cognitive Assessment System. *American Journal on Mental Retardation, 106,* 359–367.

National Alliance of Black School Educators & Council for Exceptional Children. (2002). *Addressing over-representation of African American students through promising practices: The pre-referral intervention process.* Arlington, VA: Council for Exceptional Children.

Ripp, A., Jean-Pierre, P., & Fergus, E. (2011). *Promising examples of RTI practices in urban schools.* New York, NY: National Center for Learning Disabilities.

Townsend, B. L., & Patton, J. M. (2000). Exploring some missing dimensions: Ethics, power, and privilege in the education of African American learners with disabilities and gifts and talents. *Teacher Education and Special Education, 23,* 1–2.

Townsend, B. L., Webb-Johnson, G., & Patton, J. M. (2003, January). Truth in labeling. *NEA Today,* pp. 1–56.

Warger, C., & Burnette, J. (2000). Five strategies to reduce overrepresentation of culturally and linguistically diverse students in special education (ED447627). ERIC/OSEP Digest #E596. Arlington, VA: ERIC Clearinghouse on Disabilities and Gifted Education.

Welner, K. (2004). Legal rights: The overrepresentation of culturally and linguistically diverse students in special education. The National Center for Culturally and Linguistically Educational Systems (NCCRES). http://www.nccrest.org/

Woodruff, D., Parrish, T., Heubert, J., Hehir, T., & Orfield, G. (2001, March 2). *New research on minorities and special education: Implications for federal law and policy. A forum brief.* Washington, DC: American Youth Policy Forum. Retrieved from http://www.aypf.org/forumbriefs/2001/fb030201.htm

Resources on Disproportionality in Behavioral Referrals

Ayers, W., Dohrn, B., & Ayers, R. (2001). *Zero tolerance.* New York, NY: The New Press.

Townsend, B. (2000). The disproportionate discipline of African American learners: Reducing school suspensions and expulsions. *Exceptional Children, 66,* 381–391.

Copyright © 2017 by Corwin. All rights reserved. Reprinted from *Solving Disproportionality and Achieving Equity: A Leader's Guide to Using Data to Change Hearts and Minds* by Edward Fergus. Thousand Oaks, CA: Corwin, www.corwin.com. Reproduction authorized only for the local school site or nonprofit organization that has purchased this book.

References

Ahram, R., & Fergus, E. (2011). Understanding disproportionality: Views in suburban schools. In A. Artiles, E. Kozleski, & F. Waitoller (Eds.), *Inclusive education: Examining equity in five continents.* Cambridge, MA: Harvard Education Press.

Ahram, R., Fergus, E., & Noguera, P. (2011). Addressing racial/ethnic disproportionality in special education: Case studies of suburban school districts. *Teachers College Record, 113*(10), 2233–2266.

Allport, G. W. (1954). *The nature of prejudice.* Reading, MA: Addison-Wesley.

Annamma, S., Connor, D., & Ferri, B. (2013): Dis/ability critical race studies (DisCrit): Theorizing at the intersections of race and dis/ability. *Race Ethnicity and Education, 16*(1), 1–31.

Anyon, J. (1983). Intersection of gender and class: Accommodation and resistance by working class and affluent females to contradictory sex role ideologies. In S. Walker & L. Barton (Eds.), *Gender, class and education* (pp. 19–37). Sussex, UK: Palmer.

Apple, M. W. (1997). Consuming the other: Whiteness, education, and cheap French fries. In M. Fine, L. Weiss, L. C., Powell, & L. M. Wong (Eds.), *Off-white: Readings on race, power, and society* (pp. 121–128). New York, NY: Routledge.

Ashenfelter, O., Collins, W. J., & Yoon, A. (2005). Evaluating the role of Brown vs. Board of Education in school equalization, desegregation, and the income of African Americans. NBER Working Paper No. 11394, JEL No. J7, I28, N32.

Bertrand, M., & Mullainathan, S. (2004). Are Emily and Greg more employable than Lakisha and Jamal? A field experiment on labor market discrimination. *American Economic Review, 94*(4), 991–1013.

Beck, A., & Muschkin, C. (2012). The enduring impact of race: Understanding disparities in student disciplinary infractions and achievement. *Sociological Perspectives, 55*(4), 637–662.

Bitterman, A., Goldring, R., & Gray, L. (2013). *Characteristics of public and private elementary and secondary school principals in the United States: Results from the 2011–12 schools and staffing survey* (NCES 2013–313). U.S. Department of Education. Washington, DC: National Center for Education Statistics. Retrieved August 27, 2015, from http://nces.ed.gov/pubsearch

Blanchett, W. J. (2006). Disproportionate representation of African American students in special education: Acknowledging the role of White privilege and racism. *Educational Researcher, 35*(6), 24–28.

Bonilla-Silva, E. (2003). Racism without racists: Color-blind racism and the persistence of racial inequality in the United States. Lanham, MD: Rowman & Littlefield.

Boske, C. (2015). Preparing school leaders to interrupt racism at various levels in educational systems. *International Journal of Multicultural Education, 17,* 121–142.

Bryan, J., Day-Vines, N., Griffin, D., & Moore-Thomas, C. (2012). The disproportionality dilemma: Patterns of teacher referrals to school counselors for disruptive behavior. *Journal of Counseling and Development, 90,* 177–190.

Campaign for Fiscal Equity, Inc. v. New York State, 100 N.Y.2d 893, 801 N.E.2d 326, 769 N.Y.S.2d 106 (2003).

Cole, B. P. (1986). The black educator: An endangered species. *Journal of Negro Education, 55,* 326–334.

Cooper, P. M. (2003). Effective white teachers of black children: Teaching within a community. *Journal of Teacher Education, 54*(5), 413–427.

Council of Chief State School Officers. (2008). *Educational leadership policy standards: ISLLC 2008.* Washington, DC: Author.

Council of State Governments Justice Center. (2011). *Breaking schools' rules: A statewide study of how school discipline relates to student's success and juvenile justice involvement.* New York, NY: Council of State Governments Justice Center.

Cox, D., Navarro-Rivera, J., & Jones, R. (2014). *Race, religion, and political affiliation of Americans' core social networks.* Retrieved from www.prri.org/research/race-religion-political-affiliation-americans-social-networks

Cross, W. E. (1991). *Shades of black: Diversity in African-American identity.* Philadelphia, PA: Temple University Press.

Datnow, A., Park, V., & Wohlstetter, P. (2007). *Achieving with data: How high performance driven school systems use data to improve instruction for elementary school students.* Los Angeles, CA: Center on Educational Governance, University of Southern California.

Davis, B., Gooden, M., & Micheaux, D. (2015). Color-blind leadership: A critical race theory analysis of the ISLLC and ELCC standards. *Educational Administration Quarterly, 51*(3), 335–371.

DiAngelo, R. J. (2010). Why Can't we all just be individuals? Countering the discourse of individualism in anti-racist education. *InterActions: UCLA Journal of Education and Information Studies,* 6(1).

DiAngelo, R. (2011). White fragility. *International Journal of Critical Pedagogy, 3*(3).

Eitzen, S., & Baca-Zinn, M. (1994). *Social problems.* Boston, MA: Allyn & Bacon.

Ethridge, S. B. (1979). The impact of 1954 *Brown v. Topeka* Board of Education decision on black educators. *Negro Educational Review, 30,* 217–232.

Executive Order No. 9981. (1948). Retrieved from https://www.trumanlibrary.org/9981.htm

Fabelo, T., Thompson, M., Plotkin, M., Carmichael, D., Marchbanks, M., & Booth, E. (2012). *Breaking school rules: A statewide study of how school discipline relates to students' success and juvenile justice involvement.* Washington, DC: The Council of State Governments Justice Center.

Feagin, J. (2000). *Racist America.* New York, NY: Routledge.

Feldman, M., & Pentland, B. (2003). Reconceptuaizing organizational routines as a source of flexibility and change. *Administrative Science Quarterly, 48,* 94–118.

Fergus, E. (2016). Social reproduction ideologies: Teacher beliefs about race and culture. In D. Connor, B. Ferri, & S. Annamma (Eds.), *DisCrit: Disability studies and critical race theory.* New York, NY: Teachers College Press.

Fergus, E., Noguera, P., & Martin, M. (2014). *Schooling for resilience.* Cambridge, MA: Harvard Education Press.

Fishbein, A., & Bunce, H. (2001). Subprime Market Growth and Predatory Lending, in housing policy in the new millennium: conference proceedings 273 (U.S. Department of Housing & Urban Dev. ed.), available at http://www.huduser.org/Publications/pdf/brd/13Fishbein.pdf

Gans, H. (1996). *The war against the poor.* New York, NY: Basic Books.

Gay, G. (2000). *Culturally responsive teaching: Theory, research, and practice.* New York, NY: Teachers College Press.

Gay, G. (2002). Preparing for culturally responsive teaching. *Journal of Teacher Education, 53*(2), 106.

Gravois, T. A., & Rosenfield. S. A. (2006). Impact of instructional consultation teams on the disproportionate referral and placement of minority students in special education. *Remedial and Special Education, 27*(1), 42–52.

Hall, M., Crowder, K., & Spring, A. (2015). Neighborhood foreclosures, racial/ethnic transitions, and residential segregation. *American Sociological Review, 80,* 526–549.

Harry, B., & Klingner, J. K. (2006). *Why are so many minority students in education? Understanding race and disability in schools.* New York, NY: Teachers College Press.

Hawkins, B. D. (1994). Casualties: Losses among Black educators were high after Brown. *Black Issues in Higher Education, 10*(23), 26–31.

Heifetz, R. A., Grashow, A., & Linsky, M. (2009) *The practice of adaptive leadership: Tools and tactics for changing your organization and the world.* Cambridge, MA: Harvard Business Review Press.

Hellerstein, J., & Neumark, D. (2008). Workplace segregation in the United States: Race, ethnicity and skill. *The Review of Economics and Statistics, 90*(3), 459–477.

Helms, J. (1990). *Black and White racial identity: Theory, research, and practice.* New York, NY: Greenwood Press.

Hoerr, T. R. (2005). *The art of school leadership.* Alexandria, VA: ASCD.

Holmes, B. J. (1990). *New strategies are needed to produce minority teachers.* Elmhurst, NJ: North Central Regional Educational Laboratory.

hooks, bell (1994). *Teaching to transgress: Education as the practice of freedom.* New York, NY: Routledge Press.

Iceland, J., Weinberg, D. H., & Steinmetz, E. (2002). *Racial and ethnic residential segregation in the United States: 1980–2000.* Washington, DC: U.S. Government Printing Office.

Irvine, J. J. (1990). *Black students and school failure: Policies, practices, and prescriptions.* Westport, CT: Greenwood Press.

Irvine, J. J., & York, D. E. (2001). Learning styles and culturally diverse students: A review of literature. In J. A. Banks & C. A. Banks (Eds.), *Handbook of research on multicultural education* (pp. 484–497). San Francisco, CA: Jossey-Bass.

Jennings, J. L. (2012). The effects of accountability system design on teachers' use of test score data. *Teachers College Record, 114*(11), 1–23.

Kahlenberg, R. (2012). *The future of school integration: Socioeconomic diversity as an education reform strategy.* New York, NY: Century Foundation Press.

Ladson-Billings, G. (1994). *The dreamkeepers: Successful teachers of African American children.* San Fransisco, CA: Jossey-Bass.

Ladson-Billings, G. (1999). Preparing teachers for diverse student populations: A critical race theory perspective. *Review of Research in Education, 24,* 211–247.

Lareau, A. (2003). *Unequal childhoods: Class, race, and family life.* Berkeley: University of California Press.

Lee, E., Menkart, D., Okazawa-Rey, M., & Teaching for Change (Organization). (2002). *Beyond heroes and holidays: A practical guide to K–12 anti-racist, multicultural education and staff development.* Washington, DC: Teaching for Change.

Legislation, Regulations, and Guidance. (2006). U.S. Department of Education. Retrieved from http://www2.ed.gov/programs/javits/legislation.html

Loving v. Virginia, 87 S. Ct. 1817; 18 L. Ed. 2d 1010 (1967).

Lucas, D., & Frazier, B. (2014). The effects of a service-learning introductory diversity course on pre-service teachers' attitudes toward teaching diverse student populations. *Academy of Educational Leadership Journal, 18*(2), 91–124.

Madon, S. J., Jussim, L., & Eccles, J. (1997). In search of the powerful self-fulfilling prophecy. *Journal of Personality and Social Psychology, 72,* 791–809.

Madon, S., Jussim, L., Keiper, S., Eccles, J., Smith, A., & Palumbo, P. (1998). The accuracy and power of sex, social class, and ethnic stereotypes: A naturalistic study in person perception. *Personality & Social Psychology Bulletin, 24*(12), 1304.

Madon, S., Smith, A., Jussim, L., Russell, D. W., Eccles, J., Palumbo, P., & Walkiewicz, M. (2001). Am I as you see me or do you see me as I am? Self-fulfilling prophecies and self-verification. *Personality and Social Psychology Bulletin, 27*, 1214–1224.

Madkins, T. (2011). The black teacher shortage: A literature review of historical and contemporary trends. *The Journal of Negro Education, 80*(3), 417–427.

Marsh, J. A. (2012). Interventions promoting educators' use of data: Research insights and gaps. *Teachers College Record, 114*(11).

Martin, R., & Dagostino-Kalniz, V. (2015). Living outside their heads: Assessing the efficacy of a multicultural course on the attitudes of graduate students in teacher education. *Journal of Cultural Diversity, 22*(2), 43–49.

Maxwell, K., Locke, A., & Scheurigh, J. (2014). The rural social justice leader: An exploratory profile in resilience. *Journal of School Leadership, 24*(3), 482–508.

McClellan, R., & Casey, P. (2015). Lost in transition? Campus leaders' professional pathways. *Journal of School Leadership, 25*(4), 720–757.

McKenzie, K. B., & Scheurich, J. J. (2004). Equity traps: A useful construct for preparing principals to lead schools that are successful with racially diverse students. *Educational Administration Quarterly, 40*(5), 601–632.

Milner, H. R. (2006). Classroom management in urban classrooms. In C. M. Evertson & C. S. Weinstein (Eds.), *The handbook of classroom management: Research, Practice & Contemporary Issues* (pp. 491–522). Mahwah, NJ: Lawrence Erlbaum.

Milner, H. R. (2010). *Start where you are but don't stay there: Understanding diversity, opportunity gaps, and teaching in today's classrooms.* Cambridge, MA: Harvard Education Press.

Murnane, R. J., Singer, J. D., Willett, J. B., Kemple, J. J., & Olsen, R. J. (1991). *Who will teach? Policies that matter.* Cambridge, MA: Harvard University Press.

National Center on Education Statistics (2004 and 2011). Schools and staffing survey. Washington, DC: U.S. Department of Education.

National Research Council. (2002). Minority students in special and gifted education (Committee on Minority Representation in Special Education, M. S. Donovan & C. T. Cross, Eds., Division of Behavioral and Social Sciences and Education). Washington, DC: National Academy Press.

Nicholson-Crotty, S., Birchmeier, Z., & Valentine, D. (2009). Exploring the impact of school discipline on racial disproportion in the juvenile justice system. *Social Science Quarterly, 90*(4), 1003–1018.

Noguera, P. A. (2003). Schools, prisons, and social implications of punishment: Rethinking disciplinary practices. *Theory into Practice, 42*, 341–350.

O'Connor, C., & Fernandez, S. (2006). Race, class and disproportionality: Reevaluating the relationship between poverty and special education placement. *Educational Researcher, 35*, 6–11.

Ondrich, J. (2003). Now you see it, now you don't: Why do real estate agents withhold available houses from black customers? *Review of Economics & Statistics, 85*, 854, 872.

Orfield, G., & Frankenberg, E. (2014). Increasingly segregated and unequal schools as courts reverse policy. *Educational Administration Quarterly, 50*(5), 718–734.

Pager, D., Western, B., & Bonikowski, B. (2009). Discrimination in a low-wage labor market: A field experiment. *American Sociological Review, 74*, 777–799.

Park, V., Daly, A., & Guerra, A. (2012). Strategic framing: How leaders craft the meaning of data use for equity and learning. *Educational Policy, 27*, 645–675.

Pettigrew, T. F. (1979). The ultimate attribution error: Extending Allport's cognitive analysis of prejudice. *Personality and Social Psychology Bulletin, 5*(4), 461–476.

Pettigrew, T. F., & Tropp, L. R. (2006). A meta-analytic test of intergroup contact theory. *Journal of Personality and Social Psychology, 90*, 751.

Pollack, T. M., & Zirkel, S. (2013). Negotiating the contested terrain of equity-focused change efforts in schools: Critical race theory as a leadership framework for creating more equitable schools. *Urban Review: Issues and Ideas in Public Education, 45*(3), 290–310.

Pollock, M., Deckman, S., Mira, M., & Shalaby, C. (2010). "But what can I do?": Three necessary tensions in teaching teachers about race. *Journal of Teacher Education, 61*(3), 211–224.

Proctor, C. P. (1984). Teacher expectations: A model for school improvement. *The Elementary School Journal, 84*(4), 468–481.

Rivera-McCutchen, R. (2014). The moral imperative of social justice leadership: A critical component of effective practice. *Urban Review, 46*(4), 747.

Singleton, G. E. (2015). *Courageous conversations about race: A field guide for achieving equity in schools.* Thousand Oaks, CA: Corwin.

Skiba, R. J., Horner, R. H., Chung, C.-G., Rausch, M. K., May, S. L., & Tobin, T. (2011). Race is not neutral: A national investigation of African American and Latino disproportionality in school discipline. *School Psychology Review, 40*(1), 85–107.

Skiba, R., Chung, C., Trachok, M., Baker, T., Sheya, A., & Hughes, R. (2014). Parsing disciplinary disproportionality: Contributions of infraction, student, and school characteristics to out-of-school suspension and expulsion. *American Educational Research Journal, 51,* 640–670.

Skiba, R. J., Michael, R. S., Nardo, A. C., & Peterson, R. L. (2002). The color of discipline: Sources of racial and gender disproportionality in school punishment. *The Urban Review, 34,* 317–342.

Skiba, R. J., Peterson, R. L., & Williams, T. (1997). Office referrals and suspension: Disciplinary intervention in middle schools. *Education and Treatment of Children, 20,* 295–315.

Soss, J., Fording, R., & Schram, S. (2011). *Disciplining the poor: Neoliberal paternalism and the persistent power of race.* Chicago, IL: University of Chicago Press.

Skiba, R., Simmons, A., Ritter, S., Kohler, K., Henderson, M., & Wu, T. (2006). The context of minority disproportionality: Practitioner perspectives on special education referral. *Teachers College Record, 108,* 1424–1459.

Spencer, M. B. (2006). Phenomenology and ecological systems theory: Development of diverse groups. In W. Damon & R. M. Lerner (Series Eds.) & R. M. Lerner (Vol. Ed.), *Handbook of child psychology: Vol. 1. Theoretical models of human development* (6th ed., pp. 829–893). New York: John Wiley.

Steele, C. M., & Aronson, J. (1995). Stereotype threat and the intellectual test performance of African Americans. *Journal of Personality and Social Psychology, 69,* 797–811.

Sue, D. W. (2010). Microaggressions, marginality and oppression. In D. W. Sue (Ed.), *Microaggressions and marginality* (pp. 3–22). Hoboken, NJ: Wiley.

Sue, D. W. (2013). Race talk: The psychology of race dialogues. *American Psychologist, 68*(8), 663–672.

Sullivan, A. R. , Klingbeil, D. A., & Van Norman, E. R. (2013). Beyond behavior: Multilevel analysis of the influence of sociodemographics and school characteristics on students' risk of suspension. *School Psychology Review, 42*(1), 99–114.

Tajfel, H. (1978). *Differentiation between social groups: Studies in the social psychology of intergroup relations.* London, UK: Academic Press.

Theohanis, G. (2008). Woven in deeply: Identity and leadership of urban social justice principals. *Education and Urban Society, 41*(l), 3–25.

Tillman, L. (2004). Unintended consequences? The impact of *Brown v. Board* on the employment status of black educators. *Education and Urban Society, 36*(3), 280–303.

Valencia, R. R. (1997). *The evolution of deficit thinking: Educational thought and practice.* London, UK: Falmer Press.

Weinstein, C. S., Thomlinson-Clarke, S., & Curran, M. (2003). Culturally responsive classroom management: Awareness into action. *Theory into Practice, 42,* 269–276.

Winkelman, P. (2012). Collaborative inquiry for equity: Discipline and discomfort. *Planning & Changing, 43*(3/4), 280–293.

Wiemelt, J., & Welton, A. (2015). Challenging the dominant narrative: Critical bilingual leadership (liderazgo) for emergent bilingual Latina students. *International Journal of Multicultural Education, 17*(1), 82–101.

Index

Adichie, Chimamanda Ngozi, 189
Administrators. *See* Leadership

Beck, A., 5
Behavioral considerations
    codes of conduct, 74–75
    impact of beliefs, 190–191
    poverty disciplining, 42–45
    student demographics, 3–6, 4 (tables)
    See also Discipline
Belief statements, 191
Belief systems. *See* Colorblindness; Deficit-
    thinking beliefs; Poverty-disciplining
    belief
Bias, dynamics of, 3–6, 167–168
    See also Colorblindness; Deficit-thinking
        beliefs; Equity based focus
        development; Poverty-disciplining
        belief
Bonilla-Silva, Eduardo, 32, 33
Brown v. Topeka Board of Education, 1,
    15 (figure), 16–17
Bryan, J., 5

Charter schools
    colorblindness and, 32–33
    no-excuses approach, 42–43
Civil Rights Act of 1964, 16, 20
Civil Rights Project, 1
Colorblindness
    charter schools and, 32–33
    cultural diversity and, 35–36,
        186–188
    examples, 34–36
    framework, 31–32
    individualism and, 33
    limitations and impacts, 184–188,
        225–227
    reflection activity, 37
    teacher self-efficacy and, 31
    White fragility, 33–34
Composition index, 81
Council of State Government Justice
    Center, 5
Cox, D., 16
Cross-cultural experiences, 16

Cultural diversity
    colorblindness and, 35–36, 185–186
    curriculum development and, 65–66
    deficit-thinking beliefs and, 38–40
    responsiveness to, 74
    social identity, 2, 7, 32, 186, 192–193
Culture of poverty model, 38–39
Curriculum. *See* Pedagogy and
    instructional practices

Data and research analysis
    assessment competency, 50
    on culturally responsive pedagogy, 65–66
    data analysis competency, 51–52
    data inventory worksheet, 198
    data process template, 152–153
    discipline patterns, 55–58, 116–118
    on gifted programs, 59–61, 100–109
    monthly data calendar, 142–151
    quantitative data tools, 80–81
    root cause analysis process overview,
        72–73, 73 (figure)
    school infrastructure and, 53
    software competency, 49
    on special education, 62–64, 86–95
    See also Root cause analysis
Day-Vines, N., 5
Deckman, S., 169
Deficit-thinking beliefs
    culture of poverty model, 38–39
    definition of, 38
    examples of, 38 (box), 39–40
    genetic pathology model, 38
    limitations and impact of, 176–179,
        206–208
    reflection activity, 41
DiAngelo, Robin, 33
Discipline
    data analysis of patterns, 55–58
    root cause analysis process and, 83,
        116–126
Discipling the Poor (Soss, Fording, &
    Schram), 42
Disproportionality
    common root causes of, 74–79
    in curriculum and instruction, 75–77

in discipline patterns, 115
in gifted programs, 100
in grading outcomes, 154–158
in referral process, 77–78
root cause analysis, 70–74, 71 (figure),
    73 (figure)
in special education, 86
See also Root cause analysis
Diversity. *See* Cultural diversity; Race,
    ethnicity, and gender

Educational Leadership Program
    Recognition Standards (ELCC), 20
Educational policy
    bias in, 27
    misalignments in, 74–75
    overview for creation of equity-driven
        school, 10–14
    referral processes and, 5–6, 77–78
    root cause analysis and, 74, 134
    See also Equity based focus development
Emotional disturbance, 88
English Language Learners (ELL), 79
Equity based focus development
    colorblindness impacts on, 184–188,
        225–227
    curriculum development, 62–64, 75–77
    data and research analysis capacity, 48
    deficit-thinking impacts on, 176–179,
        206–208
    definitions of educational equity,
        171–173, 201–204
    discipline patterns analysis, 55–59
    equity principles, 170–175, 199, 205
    gifted programs, 59–61
    goal-setting process for, 135–141
    grading outcomes, 159–165
    overview of, 10–14
    poverty-disciplining impacts on,
        179–183, 210–211
    progress-monitoring tools, 142–153
    race dialogue management, 168–170
    resources and activities for, 189–195
    root cause analysis and, 72–73,
        73 (figure), 134
    social identity affirmations, 192–195
    special education, 62–64, 77–78
    See also Disproportionality
Ethnicity. *See* Race, ethnicity, and gender

Feldman, M., 30
Fergus, Edward, 201
Fernandez, S., 43
Fording, Richard, 42
Frankenburg, E., 18

Gans, Herbert, 168
Gender. *See* Race, ethnicity, and gender
Genetic pathology model, 38
Gifted and talented programs

data analysis on, 59–61
root cause analysis process and, 84,
    100–114
student demographics, 3, 4 (table)
Goal-setting process
    goal identity, 135
    indicators, 136–137
    task list, 138
    timeline, 139–141
Grading outcomes
    course grade worksheets, 154–158
    monthly gradebook audit, 159–165
Griffin, D., 5

Hellerstein, J., 17
Henderson, M., 5
Hobson, Mellody, 189
Hoerr, Thomas, 170
hooks, bell, 16
Housing integration, 16–17
Hypersegregation, 18

IDEA 2004, 75, 78, 86
Identity, social, 2, 7, 32, 186, 192–193
Immigration Act of 1924, 38
Implicit Association Test, 189
Individual Education Plans (IEPs), 5
Individualism and marginalization, 33
Integration project overview
    diversification, importance of, 27
    principal demographics, 24–27,
        25 (figures), 26 (figures)
    student demographics, 17–20,
        18 (figure), 19 (figure)
    teacher demographics, 20–24,
        22 (figure), 23 (figures), 24 (figure)
Interstate School Leaders Licensure
    Consortium (ISLLC), 20
Intervention strategies, 74–77, 96–97

Kohler, K., 5

Ladson-Billings, Gloria, 201
Leadership
    building equity principles, 170–175,
        199, 205
    management of race dialogues, 168–170
    root cause analysis team, 80
    self-assessment activities, 49–54
Learning disability. *See* Special education
Lee, Enid, 201

Marginalization and individualism, 33
McKenzie, K. B., 31
Meritocracy line exercise, 212–213
Microaggressions, 17
Milner, H. Richard, 201
Mira, M., 169
Moore-Thomas, C., 5
Muschkin, C., 5

Name Game, 190
National Center on Education Statistics, 18
Neumark, D., 17
New York State Center on
    Disproportionality, 74

O'Connor, C., 43
Orfield, G., 18
Organizational processes
    ostensive component, 30
    performative component, 30

PBS, 189–190
Pedagogy and instructional practices
    colorblindness and, 31–37
    culturally responsive, 65–66, 74, 75
    disproportionality in, 74, 75–77
    identity affirmation in, 192–195
Pentland, B., 30
Pollock, M., 169
Poverty. *See* Socioeconomic status
Poverty-disciplining belief
    components of, 42–43
    examples of, 43–44
    limitations and impacts of, 179–183,
        210–211
    reflection activity, 45
President's Committee on Equality of
    Treatment and Opportunity in the
    Armed Services, 16
Principals, demographics of, 21, 24–27,
    25 (figures), 26 (figures)
Professional development
    classroom dialogue management
        strategies, 168–170
    cultural responsiveness, 79–80
    curriculum development, 76
    equity principles, 171–175
Professional Learning Communities
    (PLCs), 30

Race, ethnicity, and gender
    behavioral referrals and, 3–6, 4 (tables)
    Brown v. Topeka Board of Education, effects
        of, 1
    classroom dialogues on, 168–170
    colorblindness, 32–36, 184–188
    culturally responsive pedagogy,
        65–66, 74
    equity principles, 170–175, 216–218
    gifted and talented programs and, 3,
        4 (table)
    housing integration, 16–17
    principal demographics, 24–27,
        25 (figures), 26 (figures)
    student demographics, 17–20,
        18 (figure), 19 (figure)
    teacher demographics, 2, 20–24,
        21 (figure), 22 (figure), 23 (figures),
        24 (figure)

workplace integration, 17
    See also Colorblindness; Cultural
        diversity
Referrals. *See* Discipline; Special education
Relative risk ratio, 81
Response to intervention (RTI), 75, 78
Risk index, 81
Ritter, S., 5
Root cause analysis
    common root causes, 74–79
    data tools, 80–85
    gifted programs, outcome data, 100–110
    gifted programs, process data, 111–114
    leadership team formation, 80
    needs determination, 70–72, 71 (figure)
    process of, 72–73, 73 (figure)
    special education, outcome data, 86–95, 99
    special education, process data, 96–99

Scheurich, J. J., 31
School environments
    bias-based beliefs in, 17
    colorblindness and, 34–37
    curriculum disproportionality, 74, 75–77
    equity principles, 173–175
    intervention strategies and, 76–77
    race dialogue management strategies,
        168–170
    root cause analysis of disproportionality,
        72–73, 73 (figure)
    social identity and, 192–193
    teacher diversity and, 20–22
    vulnerability in, 183, 214–215
    See also Equity based focus development
Schram, Sandford, 42
Self-efficacy, 17, 31
Shalaby, C., 169
Simmons, A., 5
Singleton, Glenn, 201
Skiba, R., 5
SMART goals. *See* Goal-setting process
Socialization and school desegregation,
    1–2
Social networks and integration, 16
Socioeconomic status
    culture of poverty model, 38–39
    special education and, 79–80
    teacher demographics and, 22–23
Soss, Joe, 42
Special education
    data and research analysis on, 62–64
    disproportionality in, 77–80, 86
    learning capacity and, 78
    referral process, 77–78
    root cause analysis, outcome data, 85,
        86–95, 99
    root cause analysis, process data, 96–99
    student demographics, 2–3, 3 (table)
State Performance Plan (SPP), 86
Stereotypes, 17

Students
    intervention programs, 74, 75–76
    racial and ethnic demographics of, 2–6,
        3 (table), 4 (tables), 17–20,
        18 (figure), 19 (tables)
    social identity, 192–193
    struggling learners, 74, 75–77
Sue, Derald Wing, 168, 169, 170
Sullivan, A. R., 5

Teachers
    colorblindness belief, 31–37
    effect of *Brown v. Topeka Board of
        Education,* 15 (figure), 16–17
    instructional capacity, 75
    professional development of, 76
    See also Pedagogy and instructional
        practices

Teacher Uses N-Word (video), 189
Technical Assistance Center on
    Disproportionality, 74
TED Talks, 189
Temporary Assistance for Needy Families
    (TANF), 42
Theory of compromised human
    development, 43
Truman, Harold, 16

U.S. Census Bureau, 16

Valencia, Richard, 38
Vulnerability, 183, 214–215

White fragility, 33–34
Workplace environments, 17
Wu, T., 5

A SAGE Publishing Company

Helping educators make the greatest impact

CORWIN HAS ONE MISSION: to enhance education through intentional professional learning.

We build long-term relationships with our authors, educators, clients, and associations who partner with us to develop and continuously improve the best evidence-based practices that establish and support lifelong learning.

Solutions you want. Experts you trust. Results you need.

AUTHOR CONSULTING

Author Consulting

On-site professional learning with sustainable results! Let us help you design a professional learning plan to meet the unique needs of your school or district. www.corwin.com/pd

INSTITUTES

Institutes

Corwin Institutes provide collaborative learning experiences that equip your team with tools and action plans ready for immediate implementation. www.corwin.com/institutes

ECOURSES

eCourses

Practical, flexible online professional learning designed to let you go at your own pace. www.corwin.com/ecourses

READ2EARN

Read2Earn

Did you know you can earn graduate credit for reading this book? Find out how: www.corwin.com/read2earn

Contact an account manager at (800) 831-6640 or visit **www.corwin.com** for more information.